Coffee with Mimi

Published by Dream Releaser Enterprises

Cover design by Eric Powell
Cover Photo by Jordan Fernandes

ISBN: 978-1-957369-12-9 1 2 3 4 5 6 7 8 9 10

Printed in the United States of America

DEBORAH STRICKLIN

Coffee with Mimi

Life-Giving Lessons To Shape the Next Generation

DREAM RELEASER PUBLISHING

OTHER BOOKS WRITTEN BY DEBORAH STRICKLIN

The Journey

Come to the Mountain

The Tempted

Sacrifice Required

In the Stillness

Enter In

Free to Love

God of Rest

Joy in Surrender
Published by Bridge Logos

Trophies of His Grace

Seeds of Faith

Dedication

Much of who I am today is due to the upbringing my parents gave me. My childhood home was a safe and loving place. Home was truly a refuge from the difficulties of life. My parents took us to church regularly and set an example of faithfulness and devotion to God. Mom and Dad provided well for me and my sister, and they never gave us a reason to doubt their love for us.

But beyond all of that, my mom had such a beautiful relationship with Christ that she easily drew others in. People simply wanted to be near her. She was full of Godly wisdom and insight, which was given freely to anyone who came close.

Mom's love for her grandchildren somehow seemed to exceed her love for her own children. But then again, by loving my children, she was loving me too! We all miss her daily influence in our family, but many of her sayings still echo in our conversations. When we are walking through intense difficulty, we remember her saying, "*This too shall pass*," reminding us that the ebb and flow of life brings both blessing and difficulty. When we're ill, we still remember the words, "*Eat and sleep, Sweetheart*," reminding us that our pace of life needs to slow down for much-needed rest. And when we're anxious to move on to the next great adventure in life, we recall her wise words, "*Most of life is lived in the mundane, so learn to enjoy each day.*"

I dedicate the words of this book to my mom and dad, Gary and Judy Warner, who laid such a solid foundation for living this life well.

Thank you for your love, your sacrifices, your faith, and your consistency. I couldn't have asked for anything more.

Contents

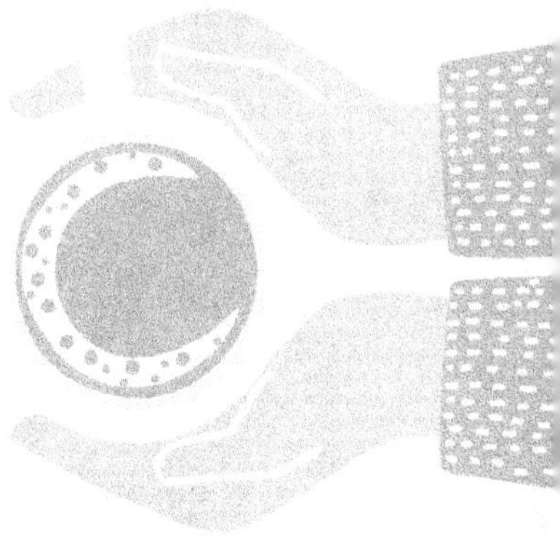

Acknowledgements

Thank you to my family for being my cheerleaders. No matter what I endeavor to do, you're right there to encourage me.

Thank you, Kirsten, for the investment of your time and talent into this project. You have a wonderful way of helping me actually say what I mean to say. And I'm so grateful. Thank you, Heather and Jonathon, for reading through the manuscript and giving me your honest feedback.

Thank you to all of our DSM Champions for partnering with us to advance the kingdom of God around the world.

And most of all, thank you to our Lord and Savior, Jesus Christ, for loving us beyond all comprehension.

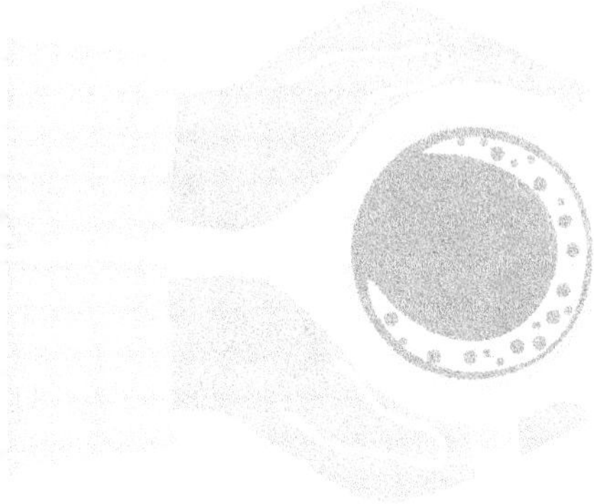

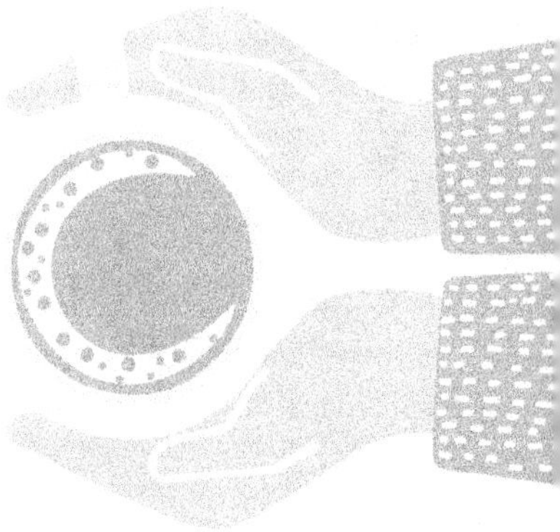

Introduction

Every so often, someone I know will share with me something impressive one of my adult children has said or done. I smile and usually answer, "They impress me, too." Inevitably, within the brief conversation, the question arises, "How did you raise *three* great kids?" This question makes me laugh for a couple of reasons: First, there's always the feeling behind such a well-meaning question that *surely* one of them should have been the reprehensible child; and secondly, there's simply no way to gather up all the prayers prayed, all the books read, all the mentoring sessions attended, and all the wisdom gleaned from the Holy Spirit into one neatly packaged answer.

So much of what I know about life I learned from my mom (Nana to my children *and* their friends). She was always there for me, ready to share a kind word of encouragement or a carefully-crafted word of correction. *Adulting*, as it's called today, wasn't so scary because I always had the safety net of a phone call to Mom. She gave me so many nuggets of wisdom over my lifetime.

Somehow, until now, it never occurred to me to write down some of these wise principles for others to read. After all, *Nana* had been the carrier of wisdom for each of us. We know that wisdom didn't begin with Nana—the

Word of God brings us wisdom—but Nana was the conduit of wisdom passed down from generations past to the current generation about all sorts of practical matters like raising children, transitioning teenagers, handling money, and just being a good human.

When I got frustrated with my young ones, I'd seek out the wise words of my mom. And when my children weren't sure that *I* had given them the right answer about a certain matter, they'd go ask Nana for themselves. Most of the time she would confirm the very words I had spoken, but there was something about Nana's stamp of approval that suddenly made *my* words acceptable to my children.

My mother's recent death left a breach in my family's flow of wisdom. I didn't realize the importance of this at first. All I saw was what we had lost, not what was to be gained through the transition of her death. As I sat talking with my neighbor one day soon after my mom's funeral, I realized it was time for me to step forward. One of my daughters was expecting her first child—my first grandchild—so there was no time to waste. It was time to repair the breach in the flow of generational wisdom and take my position as *Mimi*.

As a grandmother, I recognize that so many young people today don't have a mom, a Nana, or a Mimi to lean on for advice and Godly counsel. God has allowed this burden to grow on my heart for many years now, and I want to help bridge that gap. I have written this book with the understanding that even though I don't have all the answers, I've been blessed with good counsel and life experiences that I'd love to share. I'd be honored to be your honorary Mimi through the pages of this book.

So, get yourself a cup of coffee, or hot tea if you prefer, and let's talk. I have so much to share with you—comforting words, teaching words, encouraging words, challenging words. My prayer for you is that you will breathe a little easier knowing you have a Mimi who wants to share Godly wisdom with you. May God richly bless you and your family as we journey through life's ups and downs together.

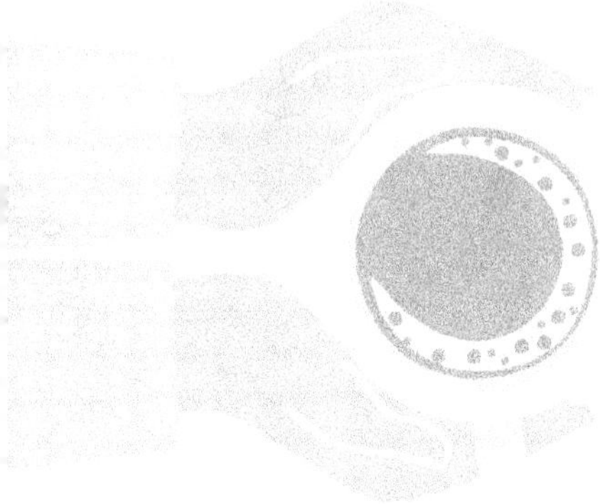

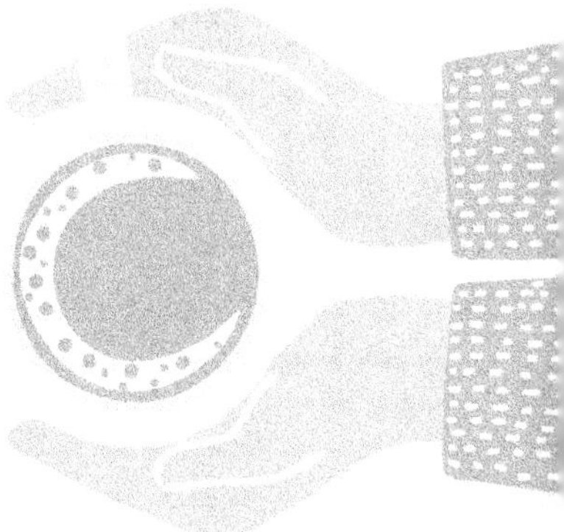

Lesson 1

Work on Yourself First

"Do as I say, not as I do." How easy life would be if we could simply tell our children what to do without actually doing it ourselves! But as we'll discuss throughout this book, very few things in life are learned without following an example.

As infants, we mimic the sounds we hear to form our first words. As we grow, we learn social cues from our parents, friends, and acquaintances. And as adults, we develop our skills by watching those who have mastered what we're attempting to learn. So, it's important for us to remember that as we're parenting (and grandparenting), our children *will* follow in our footsteps. They will make their choices based on watching what choices we make.

I remember when my third child, Jonathon, was born. Kirsten was four years old, and Heather was three. We had a green hand-me-down recliner in which I rocked each of my babies, and I prayed as I rocked them for hours in that chair. I remember asking God one day when Jonathon was just a newborn baby, "How do I teach them to love You, Lord?" His reply was so profoundly simple, "*Let Me lead you, and they will follow.*"

Those words from the Lord have guided me in every step of parenting as well as in every other aspect of my life. The principle is simple and consistently true: the best way to influence others is to *be* the right example in front of them. For instance, when we are honest, we silently encourage others to be honest. When we are kind, we encourage others to be kind. When we develop a passionate and intimate relationship with Christ, we inspire others to do the same.

> *The best way to influence others is to be the right example in front of them.*

Our children will be influenced most by who we are, not by who we want them to be or what we want them to do. So it's critical that we allow God to shape our characters through His Word and through relationship with Him. Because of God's words spoken to me that day when Jonathon was just a newborn baby, I knew that if I kept letting God work on my heart and transform my thinking, my children would learn to let God lead their lives as well.

This is a counterintuitive way of thinking—to indirectly instruct our children through our own example. We naturally want to simply tell our children to be honest, less selfish, or more giving. But if we'll be a little less vocal and a little more humbly influential by letting God work on *us*, we'll see the results we're looking for in our children.

My middle child, Heather, has always been the one who looks and acts most like me. We share many personality traits and tend to operate in similar giftings. This can be a wonderful compliment to a mother—having a daughter that is a mirror image of herself. But let's be honest. As women, we tend to exhibit jealousy and competitive behavior when we're around other women who are too similar. It's as if we believe there isn't enough room in the world for both of us.

When Heather was about eight years old, I was daily faced with this spitting image of myself, and I remember being so shocked that she kept exhibiting negative traits like arrogance and selfish independence. And to no avail, I kept trying to correct her behavior with harsh words and punishment.

Finally, I took the matter to prayer. Frustrated, exhausted, and ready to lock Heather in her room for the next ten years, I cried out to God to change this wayward child of mine. His reply makes me smile as I look back on my completely ill-chosen request. He rather pointedly said, "*She's only copying what she sees you do.*"

Ouch! That was God's grace-filled way of saying I needed to work on myself. I suppose His reply could have been deeply insulting had I not realized that God was actually helping me. So I began focusing on letting God correct the negative traits in *my* life that I saw reflected in my daughter. I was amazed that as I changed, so did Heather. Then the Lord instructed me, "*Let her be a mirror for you. If you see something in her that needs to change, change it in yourself.*"

Instead of arguing with my *mini-me*, I allowed Heather's behavior to become an indicator of what was happening in my own heart. Rather than succumbing to the natural reaction of holding her at arm's length, I drew her close. My love for Heather has only grown because of this symbiotic relationship—she directs my attention to my need for change, and as I change, she follows my example.

Jesus Himself demonstrated this model of *being the example* for others. He humbly chose to leave Heaven, be born as a baby, live without sin, and die on a cross. He showed us how to live here on Earth and grant us access to eternal life with Him. And as we follow Christ's example, others can follow us.

The apostle Paul, in his letter to the Philippian believers in Christ, said, "*Dear brothers and sisters, pattern your lives after mine, and learn from those who follow our example*" (Philippians 3:17, NLT). This is the essence of the Christian life: to live in such a way that others can follow us to the cross of Jesus Christ and there find *true Life*. And we continue to grow in Christ-likeness as we seek to know Him and His Word better and better.

As we pursue being more like Christ, those who are closely connected to our lives—particularly our children—are unmistakably influenced by our transformative growth. And if we will view raising our children as an opportunity to grow right along with them, it's a win-win situation. Our growth causes us to become more like Christ, and *we* become our children's best example.

FOCUS QUESTIONS:

1) Think of a positive instance when your children or grandchildren copied something you did. Now, think of a negative instance. Did those experiences change your behavior? Why or why not?

____

____

____

____

____

2) What actions or habits do you want your children/grandchildren to develop as adults? What can you do now to model those actions?

PRAYER

Father, help me draw closer to You each day and to allow Your Word and Your Holy Spirit to transform me. And as I become more like You, please let me be an example of Your love and grace to my children and my grandchildren. Amen.

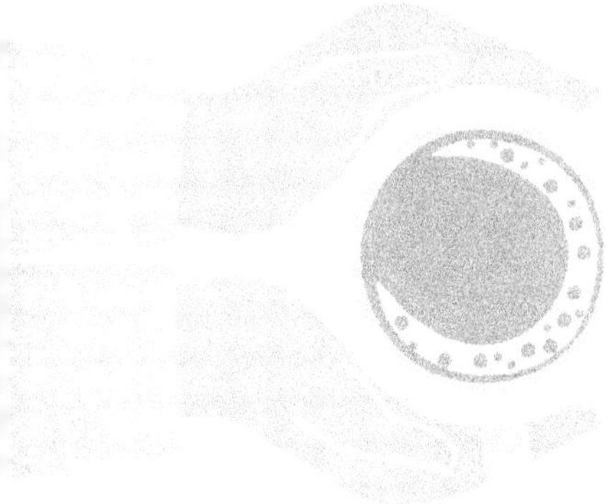

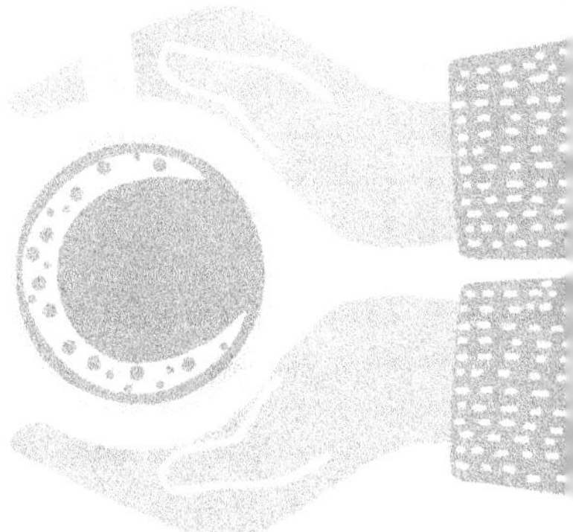

Lesson 2

Create an Atmosphere of Unconditional Love

There is something incredibly powerful about creating an atmosphere of unconditional love with your life, and especially within your own family. This doesn't mean you are accepting of wrong behavior; it means you choose to willingly love the person behind the wrong behavior. My mom was especially good at conveying unconditional love. She had a way of showing even the "worst transgressor" that they were loved.

Toward the end of her life, she gave sage grandmotherly advice to my sister, many of our friends, and me, knowing that we would one day soon have our own grandchildren. She would say, "As a grandma, don't correct too sternly. Hold their hands, look face to face, talk about it. If Grandma is mad at them, they don't have a friend left in the world."

And of course, this isn't just good advice for grandmothers. Even as an adult, I remember calling Mom for a voice of reassurance when it seemed there wasn't anyone left in my corner. Although she wasn't always able to hold my hands or talk face to face, her love was felt by the words she spoke. I knew Mom would be there for me—she always was.

God put us in families for a reason. He knew that if we would invest in one another by loving and serving each other, we would create strong relational bonds that are not easily broken. So as we raise our young ones, we naturally develop a profound love for them—a love that is able to see past their momentary unwise decisions and wrong actions.

This is what God does for us. As we read His Word and attempt to implement His way of doing things, we make mistakes. We get our eyes off Him occasionally and make selfish decisions. But He is there to speak a corrective word and get us back on track.

One of the clearest Biblical examples of God's unconditional love is in the book of Jonah. God gave Jonah specific instructions to warn the people of Nineveh that His judgment was coming upon the people of that evil city. Jonah didn't want to deliver the message to Nineveh and—selfishly—set off in the opposite direction. Through an almost unbelievable series of events involving a very large fish, Jonah finally relented and delivered God's message to the city of Nineveh. Miraculously, the people there heard God's warning and repented. God saw their repentance and stayed His hand of judgment. What incredible mercy! However, Jonah was unhappy because God's judgment didn't come to pass. Jonah wanted to be right more than he wanted to see the people of Nineveh saved from destruction. God exposed Jonah's selfishness, yet God showed Jonah unconditional love through forgiveness and second chances. His desire is always relationship, no matter how far we run.

In the same way, when we approach God, He invites us to move toward Him because His love for us willingly draws us back into relationship with Him. One of the most beautiful verses about the depth of God's love for us is found in Romans 8:38-39 (ESV): *"For I am sure that neither death nor life, nor angels nor rulers, nor things present nor things to come, nor powers, nor height nor depth, nor anything else in all creation, will be able to separate us from the love of God in Christ Jesus our Lord."*

Our challenge, and responsibility, is to follow His example—to produce an atmosphere of unconditional love with our lives. Children will learn much about the attributes of God by their interactions with their parents. For example, if parents are generous with their time and resources, children tend to grow up believing God is generous toward them. If parents are distracted and uninterested in their children's activities, children tend to believe that God is distant and uninvolved in the details of our lives.

If parents don't set firm boundaries for their children's behavior and follow through with discipline, children emerge as adults with a poor understanding of God's power. They tend to believe that He is easily manipulated. We, as parents (and grandparents), truly establish in our children their foundational beliefs about God.

Our challenge, and responsibility, is to follow His example—to produce an atmosphere of unconditional love with our lives.

In my dad's older years, he has become increasingly protective of his family. Now that his focus has shifted away from earning an income, he often actively searches for ways to serve his children and grandchildren. I remember several years ago when my daughter Kirsten and I were visiting Mom and Dad when they lived in Santa Barbara. Kirsten and I decided to go for a run, and part way through our mileage, we discovered that my dad had been driving along our route to make sure we didn't get lost and were safe. Much like God constantly watching over us even when we're unaware, Daddy was doing just that. There are a lot of things in life that my dad didn't have control over (like my mom walking through cancer), but that one thing he could do—watch over his daughter and granddaughter. It was his way of demonstrating love.

When problems arise in life—and they consistently do—we want our children to run *to God*, not away from Him. And the best way to encourage this response to life's troubles is to help our children accept and walk in God's unconditional love. We can only do that through being an example of unconditional love toward our children.

Let me say it again—unconditional love is deeply loving the person, not excusing poor or sinful behavior. We'll talk about rewarding good behavior and properly punishing bad behavior in other lessons, but loving the person transcends both.

FOCUS QUESTIONS:

1) Did you grow up feeling unconditionally loved by your parents? If so, what made you feel loved? If not, what made you feel unloved?

____

____

____

____

____

2) How can you be more intentional about creating an atmosphere of unconditional love in your home?

PRAYER

Father, teach me more about Your love for me so I can truly love others.

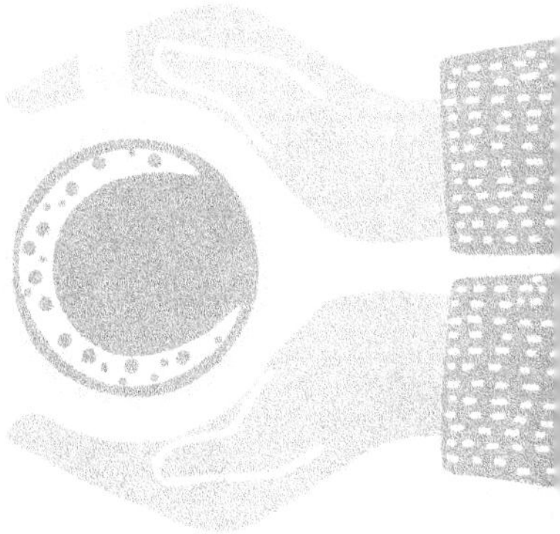

Lesson 3

Train Them to Cast Their Cares

I vividly remember the days just before my oldest daughter Kirsten started kindergarten. Although my husband and I had enrolled her in a private Christian school near our home, I felt as if I were sending her off to college halfway across the nation (which we did thirteen years later). But as a young child, she had never been apart from me for more than about three hours at a time. As I allowed my concern about sending her to school to grow larger, I asked myself, *How will she make it through a whole day of school away from home?* I realize this sounds a little silly now, but I was honestly processing that thought at the time.

As a stay-at-home mom and a teacher by profession, I had poured myself into raising my babies. Their preschool years were filled with learning opportunities and carefully crafted life lessons. I rarely do anything half-heartedly, and parenting my young children was certainly no exception. With so much of myself and my time invested in my three children, sending my oldest child off to school required a level of trust I had not yet encountered.

As I thought about how Kirsten would feel being away from home all day at school, anxiety began to consume me. *Will she be scared? As a responsible, loving parent, how could I possibly put her in that situation?* My worry was winning out over my peace. Taking my concerns to the Lord is a common practice for me, so I prayed this seemingly noble prayer: "Lord, I don't want Kirsten to be afraid when she goes to school, so please put all of her concerns on me. I'll carry them for her."

Apparently, God thought this was a great time to answer my prayer and teach me an object lesson at the same time. The anxiety I allowed to penetrate my thinking began to affect me physically. I quickly developed stomach discomfort, which turned into unexplainable, acute pain. My husband put me in the car and drove me to the local hospital's emergency room. After several tests and no explanation for the pain, the ER doctor simply sent me home. At this point, I still hadn't made the mental connection between my prayer and my circumstances.

The next evening was kindergarten orientation at the school. We dropped off our younger two children at the babysitter's house and headed to the school. I remember being barely functional—the pain was still consistently present. At the end of the evening, we picked up our children and headed home. The pain in my stomach was getting worse, so my husband drove me to the emergency room for round two. Again, the ER doctor sent me home with no explanation and no remedy.

> Our physical bodies were not created to function under the weight of fear, anxiety, and worry. We were created to fully trust God with every part of our lives.

Finally, with no other option available, I got on my knees and begged God to explain what was happening to me. His answer significantly shifted my thinking from that moment forward. He said, *"Your shoulders aren't big enough to carry the burden. You were not designed for that. Cast your cares on Me."*

His message to me was clear—by asking that Kirsten's anxieties be placed on me, I had assumed a position that was not mine to take. He alone is the *burden-bearer*. Our physical bodies were not created to function under the weight of fear, anxiety, and worry. We were created to fully trust God with every part of our lives.

As God's children, our job is to cast our cares on Him. As a matter of fact, God's Word *instructs* us not to worry.

"Give all your worries and cares to God, for he cares about you."
(1 Peter 5:7, NLT)

"Give your burdens to the LORD, and he will take care of you. He will not permit the godly to slip and fall."
(Psalm 55:22, NLT)

"Don't worry about anything; instead, pray about everything. Tell God what you need, and thank him for all he has done."
(Philippians 4:6, NLT)

"Seek the Kingdom of God above all else, and live righteously, and he will give you everything you need. So don't worry about tomorrow, for tomorrow will bring its own worries. Today's trouble is enough for today."
(Matthew 6:33-34, NLT)

Rather than focusing on our own concerns—our worries—God desires that we focus on Him and His love for us. And as we learn to dwell in God's love, fear has no place to reside inside our hearts (see 1 John 4:18).

In my own Christian walk, I was slowly learning to dwell in God's love and to cast my cares on Him. I knew that this was the answer to living without anxious thoughts. And I knew that my children needed to learn this lesson early in their young lives. So I began to teach my children that God's Word has the answers we need to live and dwell in Him.

When they would come to me for answers to their adolescent questions, I would lovingly direct them to the Bible. I would help them find the right chapter and verses, but I encouraged them to go into their rooms and read the full context of the passage. Then, they were welcome to come to me to discuss what they had read and how God's Word could be applied to their situations.

As I watched them practice this skill of consulting God's Word and then applying His wisdom to their lives, I was pleased that they were indeed learning to cast their cares on God. My children were maturing, following my example as God had so faithfully been teaching me. What a privilege to train my children to trust Him more fully!

In the process of parenting, we're often curious to see if our children will continue what they've learned from us even after they've moved away. Regarding my children's adult lives, I can say yes, they have learned to go to God's Word for answers and to cast their cares on the One who is trustworthy!

One particular incident comes to mind concerning my children's reliance on the Lord. Kirsten spent her college years eight hours away from home at a wonderful Christian university. She developed deep friendships that have lasted beyond the college environment, and she grew steadily in wisdom and academic knowledge. One day in the middle of the school semester, I got a phone call from Kirsten that was a bit concerning. She said she hadn't been feeling well and went to the health clinic to be evaluated. It was official; she had the flu. With prescription in hand, she made her way to the local drugstore to have the prescription filled. But our family's insurance company wouldn't pay for the flu medicine that the doctor had prescribed. Paying for it out-of-pocket was going to cost a bundle, and Kirsten couldn't afford to pay for it on her own. We were personally in the middle of a very difficult financial situation, so I couldn't help, either.

Looking back now, I'm tempted to feel like an irresponsible parent, but a boldness rose up inside of me at the moment she told me the amount. I said, "That's ridiculous! Go back to your dorm room and have your roommates lay hands on you and pray for you." She told the pharmacy clerk she didn't need the prescription, went back to her dorm room, and asked her roommates to pray for her. They did, and within twenty-four hours she was back in class with no fever, no weakness, and no signs of sickness. I wish I could say I had super-faith, but I honestly just had to throw myself at Jesus' feet. I was eight hours away and couldn't help her. But because she experienced God's healing power for herself, her faith grew even stronger.

Our objective as Christian parents and grandparents is to point our kids toward Jesus and encourage them to walk toward Him. We train them to cast their cares on God. And He will take care of the rest.

FOCUS QUESTIONS:

1) Do you have the tendency to worry? What causes you the greatest concern regarding your children or grandchildren?

2) We can't teach our children to cast their cares on the Lord if we don't do it ourselves. This spiritual discipline takes time to develop, so don't be afraid to start small! How can you be more intentional about giving your cares to God this week?

PRAYER

Father, teach me to look to you for help. When I start to fret, remind me to cast my cares on You.

Lesson 4

Reward Desirable Behavior

The twenty-eighth chapter of the book of Deuteronomy is broken down into two sections. The first section records the blessings for walking in obedience to the Lord, and the second section records the curses for disobeying the Lord. I've always appreciated how God lays out His expectations for us so clearly.

My personality lends itself to seeing things in a very black and white manner—literal and straight-forward. So, God's method of matter-of-fact communication speaks clearly to me. And as my children were growing up, I used this method (and these Biblical chapters) to help them understand that blessings follow obedience. If I sensed that one of them was about to choose to disobey, I would hold out both of my hands, palms facing up, and like an invisible scale weighing their choices, I would say, "Obedience – blessing. Disobedience – curses. You choose."

I guess that could be interpreted as a little harsh, but it was effective! Although I spoke very few words at those moments, they quickly got the picture and most often made the right choice. By the time our children were in their teenage years, they no longer needed me to even speak those words. They simply understood the important choice that was ever present before them.

As Christian parents, we must help our children make the connection between *right behavior* and reward. Since God makes that connection for us in His Word, we must do the same with our children. *Right behavior* is godly obedience even when we don't understand the reason behind the instructions.

> *As Christian parents, we must help our children make the connection between right behavior and reward.*

I remember a specific phone conversation with my oldest daughter Kirsten that tested her resolve to obey despite her lack of understanding. She was a senior in high school at the time, and she wanted to go line dancing in a well-known Nashville bar with a group of her friends. My mobile phone rang just as I pulled into the parking lot of the Christian private school where I was teaching fifth grade and where she was attending.

As Kirsten told me of her plans, I quieted myself internally and waited until she finished. Her explanation was thorough, and she gave compelling reasons why her excursion would be innocent of any *wrong behavior*. However, as a parent with a bit more experience in life, I told her I didn't think it was a good idea. Silence ensued. I could tell she was wrestling with what I wanted her to do versus what she wanted to do. She was eighteen years old and about to graduate from high school, and although I had the parental authority to lay down the law, I knew I no longer had the leverage to back it up. I knew I had to rely on all I taught her over the years and on the relationship we had developed.

She tried once more to reason her way into changing my mind, but my answer remained the same. I knew because of her inexperience she couldn't see the reasons behind my answer, but I also knew that I truly had her best interest at heart by advising her not to go. Then, the shift happened. I heard it in her voice. She said she didn't really understand, but if I didn't think she should go, then she wouldn't.

Undetected by Kirsten, I breathed a huge sigh of relief and then told her that I was proud of the way she submitted to my decision. I knew she wasn't happy, but she had chosen rightly. And God's blessings on Kirsten's life have been abundant, not just for that moment of decision, but for her consistently humble and submissive attitude.

There's a beautiful passage of Scripture in Psalm 19 written by King David that reminds us to pursue God's ways and the benefits that follow:

> *The instructions of the Lord are perfect,*
> *reviving the soul.*
> *The decrees of the Lord are trustworthy,*
> *making wise the simple.*
> *The commandments of the Lord are right,*
> *bringing joy to the heart.*
> *The commands of the Lord are clear,*
> *giving insight for living.*
> *Reverence for the Lord is pure,*
> *lasting forever.*
> *The laws of the Lord are true;*

each one is fair.
They are more desirable than gold,
even the finest gold.
They are sweeter than honey,
even honey dripping from the comb.
They are a warning to your servant,
a great reward for those who obey them.

King David called God's instructions *a great reward for those who obey them.* How are they a great reward? According to this passage, they revive us, make us wise, bring us joy, and grant us insight. He also said that they will last forever and that they are fair, sweeter than honey, and more desirable than gold. Those are powerful and enticing words regarding God's commandments and their benefits to us.

Our ability to transfer the understanding of these benefits to our children starts with understanding them ourselves. Remember what I said in Lesson 1 about my conversation with God concerning raising my children? He said, *"Let Me lead you, and they'll follow."*

What if successful Christian parenting has more to do with stewarding our own relationship with God rather than pushing or dragging our children into making religiously acceptable choices? Do we really believe and live as if King David's words are true? God's ways are good and pleasant. When we, as parents, live in that truth, there is a peace and sense of God's presence that permeates our lives. And our children perceive it. Like a magnet attracts, our submitted lives will attract our children's attention. And then they will follow.

In many ways, this approach to parenting is counterintuitive. We want to simply tell our children what to do and expect them to follow our instructions. And there are times we must use that approach. But God most often leads His children with love and His own selfless example—He always has. We would do well to follow His lead as we parent our children.

> *Help your children see the reward in pursuing God's ways of doing things.*

Knowing that following God's ways brings such great reward, I encouraged my children to read the Bible. As a matter of fact, I considered reading God's Word such a worthy endeavor that I paid them to do it! Once they became excellent readers, I offered them a sum of money—that was significant to them at the time—for reading the New Testament. They could take as long as they wanted, and the offer didn't expire until they left home for college. I offered an even larger sum of money for reading the Old Testament since it was longer and more difficult to read. Although I can't know for sure whether that incentive provided the motivation to continue reading God's Word, today they are avid Bible readers. Somewhere along the way, they made the transition from a monetary motivation to a more passionate pursuit. I consider that success!

Whatever method you choose to encourage Bible reading in your home, help your children see the reward in pursuing God's ways of doing things. Reading the Bible is the only way for your children to determine the difference between right and wrong, and it's the only way to know how passionately God values obedience. *Right behavior* most certainly brings great reward.

FOCUS QUESTIONS:

1) Examine yourself. Do you read the Bible consistently? Do you personally prioritize obedience to God, even when it's not convenient?

2) Do you tend to focus on rewarding good behavior or punishing bad behavior? How can you help your children or grandchildren see the spiritual benefit of obeying God?

PRAYER

Father, teach me to obey You with a willing heart. And, Lord, continue to increase my hunger for Your Word.

Lesson 5

Purposefully Teach Delayed Gratification

As we teach our children that *right behavior* produces reward, it is also important to help them understand the concept of delayed gratification. In Western culture, we have become accustomed to immediate results, and that mindset can easily create an expectation of immediate reward for right behavior. Sometimes we, in fact, do experience reward immediately following right behavior, but more often than not, our reward comes in the form of Biblical blessing over time. Another phrase for the concept of delayed gratification might be spiritual endurance.

Nearly everything about our spiritual lives takes time to develop and grow. Teaching our children the required patience for such development and growth will be an invaluable lesson as they mature. Delayed gratification—or spiritual endurance—is a combination of actively working and waiting on the Lord. 2 Peter 1:2-11 (NLT) is one of my favorite passages regarding growth in spiritual endurance:

May God give you more and more grace and peace as you grow in your knowledge of God and Jesus our Lord.

By his divine power, God has given us everything we need for living a godly life. We have received all of this by coming to know him, the one who called us to himself by means of his marvelous glory and excellence. And because of his glory and excellence, he has given us great and precious promises. These are the promises that enable you to share his divine nature and escape the world's corruption caused by human desires.

In view of all this, make every effort to respond to God's promises. Supplement your faith with a generous provision of moral excellence, and moral excellence with knowledge, and knowledge with self-control, and self-control with patient endurance, and patient endurance with godliness, and godliness with brotherly affection, and brotherly affection with love for everyone.

The more you grow like this, the more productive and useful you will be in your knowledge of our Lord Jesus Christ. But those who fail to develop in this way are shortsighted or blind, forgetting that they have been cleansed from their old sins.

So, dear brothers and sisters, work hard to prove that you really are among those God has called and chosen. Do these things, and you will never fall away. Then God will give you a grand entrance into the eternal Kingdom of our Lord and Savior Jesus Christ.

There is a sense of divine partnership in our spiritual growth. We put effort into our knowledge, understanding, and application of God's Word, and God graces us with insight and maturity. But that insight and maturity doesn't happen overnight. We must be patient as God leads us through the growth process. So, how do we teach our children to actively work toward growing their spiritual endurance and yet patiently wait on God? Especially when they are young, we can use concrete objects to teach an abstract concept like delayed gratification (spiritual endurance).

Money is one tool that assisted us as parents to help our children think in terms of delayed gratification. As our children were growing up in our home, my husband and I consistently gave them a weekly allowance. They were required to complete chores, so they "earned" their allowance. But it wasn't just about working to earn money (although that's an important lesson). They needed access to money of their own to learn the value of saving over time to purchase something that they really wanted to buy. I remember my young ones purchasing a sucker or a candy bar with the few coins they had in their pockets on our frequent trips to the grocery store. They were so proud of their ability to choose an item they wanted and pay for it themselves. As they got a little older, they began to identify bigger, more expensive items they wanted to purchase. I still have an ornament that all three of them pooled their money to buy us one Christmas. What a treasure! But one by one, each child set their sights on a large purchase and determined to save enough to buy it.

> Delayed gratification—or spiritual endurance—is a combination of actively working and waiting on the Lord.

Sometimes, saving enough required weeks of tucking money away. Other times, it took months. Once they determined they'd saved enough, we went to the store to make the purchase.

Side Note: Parents, this is a critical moment in your child's understanding about the nature of God. If they've worked hard to save the money, and the purchase at the checkout leaves them a little short, make up the difference. Reward them for their persistent saving. God's grace covers our miscalculations, and the checkout counter is not the time to enforce an object lesson about figuring tax or properly calculating sales percentages. Your children have diligently done their best; reward them for their investment in delayed gratification. Teach about sales percentages and taxes after you get home.

By allowing them to identify a desired item, save enough to buy it, and make the purchase, you are teaching them delayed gratification. And the spiritual parallel is being solidified in the process. We lean into God's Word, and over time with much practice, He produces growth in our lives.

Physical fitness is also a means of teaching delayed gratification in our children's lives. Developing the habit of exercising regularly can be daunting, but we all know that living a lifestyle of fitness requires that we persist.

As my children were growing up, I enrolled them in the sport of their choice. My only requirements were that they follow the instructions of the coach or teacher and that they remain in the same sport for at least six months. Psychologists tell us that it takes at least three months to develop a new habit. And it usually takes at least that long to develop the skill set needed to participate in their sport of choice. I wanted them to stay in the sport long enough to know if they truly enjoyed it, and if it was a team sport, that length of time usually got them through the season.

There is one more important aspect of encouraging our children to be physically fit; we must model it for them. I wanted (and still want) my children to see what a lifestyle of physical fitness looks like, so I have made physical activity a priority in my own life. I was a competitive gymnast in my teen years, and I value the positive impact physical fitness can make in our lives.

In an effort to be an example to my children as well as enjoy the benefits of being physically active, I continued aerobic exercise throughout the years of raising my kids. And as my children grew older, they joined me in running races, biking, and swimming. These days, we compete in triathlons, play tennis, and take walks. I call it *playing together*. And as we're playing, we're reaping the benefits of having worked hard to become physically fit. We're enjoying the reward of delayed gratification—spiritual and physical endurance.

In addition to using money and physical fitness to teach this spiritual lesson, learning a new skill can also help solidify the concept. I required each of my children to learn to play a musical instrument as they were growing up. They did not need to master it; I just wanted them to understand two concepts through the process of learning to play the instrument: 1) Practicing over and over again brings proficiency, and 2) Learning to overcome frustration is part of life. Of course, learning to read music and developing an ear for musical definition are also important, but those weren't really my main objectives.

Our goal should be to help our children develop spiritual endurance, and developing delayed gratification can be the physical representation of this spiritual principle.

None of us are experts at just about anything (except selfishness) until we learn to practice. The willingness to practice is in many ways an admission of humility. We generally have to spend many hours practicing a skill in order to master it. Someone who is learning to play a musical instrument usually doesn't have the pleasure of playing without great effort until time is spent mastering the instrument. The hardest work must be exerted up front in order to enjoy effortless play. So this is a form of delayed gratification.

The second concept practiced by learning a musical instrument is that learning to overcome frustration is part of life. I remember sitting in

Heather's piano lessons and listening to the teacher gently correct Heather's timing or emphasis on certain notes. These were difficult concepts for a young child to grasp, and at times, I could see Heather's utter frustration on her face. Over and over again, she'd play the keys wrong, and her teacher would correct her and demonstrate the proper way the musical selection was to be played. Inevitably, though, I would see the mounting frustration give way to submission and determined effort to play the piece correctly.

Likewise, spiritually speaking, we tend to fight God for our own way. Amid our growing frustration, He invites us to simply submit our will to His and allow Him to lead us into closer relationship with Himself. This cycle of frustration and then submission helps train us to yield our will to His and accept His way of doing things in our lives.

Ask the Holy Spirit to show you unique methods of teaching delayed gratification in your children's lives. Our goal should be to help our children develop spiritual endurance, and developing delayed gratification can be the physical representation of this spiritual principle.

FOCUS QUESTIONS:

1) Can you think of a few specific ways to practice delayed gratification with your children or grandchildren?

____

____

____

____

2) Do you find that you personally struggle with delayed gratification from God? How can you increase your own spiritual endurance?

PRAYER

Father, help me see beyond the immediate. Teach me to practice delayed gratification in my own life. And help me to lead my children and grandchildren in working hard at something today in order to enjoy the benefits of it later.

Lesson 6

Punish Undesirable Behavior

Just as God rewards *right behavior*, He is faithful to punish *wrong behavior*. I use the word faithful because God is very clear in His Word that He cannot allow us—because of His love for us—to continue in wrong behavior.

> *My child, don't reject the LORD's discipline, and don't be upset when he corrects you. For the LORD corrects those he loves, just as a father corrects a child in whom he delights.*
> (Proverbs 3:11-12, NLT)

Because of our human propensity to sin, we are *not* naturally selfless and giving toward others. We must develop these and other positive attributes through training, which begins in the parent-child relationship. And these lessons are meant to be taught in the atmosphere of a loving, stable home environment.

When we hear the word punishment, we tend to think of harsh physical abuse. But punishment used as correction in the context of love can produce lasting *right behavior*. However, punishment can easily move toward abuse when it is exacted in anger and meted out in inappropriate measure. So, we need some guidelines to help us use punishment in a positive manner—as purposeful discipline and meaningful correction.

> Punishment used as correction in the context of love can produce lasting right behavior.

We've probably all heard, "Don't discipline your children when you're angry," which is easier said than done. If your child disobeys, you're understandably frustrated that they didn't listen to your instruction. But if you react in anger, you're *frustrated with yourself* as well as with your child. How do we approach their disobedience differently? The answer doesn't lie in simply cooling off before you discipline. There's much more to it than that. Let's explore what's going on behind the feelings of anger and frustration.

Probably the biggest hindrance to proper discipline is our own skewed view of parenting. We tend to see our children as reflections of ourselves, and if they act incongruently with our self-governing rules, then they're out of line and deserve punishment. But our children are not small versions of us. They are unique individuals created by God, given to us to steward while they're young. If we can see them in this way, then our role is to mentor these small ones and help them grow into adults who will follow and obey *the Lord's commands*, not ours. So the question is, are we training our children to conform to our image or to God's? If we're focused on training them to adhere to the Word of God, then our household rules will reflect God's rules.

For example, obedience in the home means children responding without delay, which is what God wants from us as well. Immediate obedience is important not because we as parents are on a power high, but because immediate obedience keeps us in the center of God's will. It offers protection over our lives. This concept is true for our children as well. As your child learns to walk and run, they often move about with disregard for their safety. They're too young to see all the imminent dangers. It's critical that your child learns to respond to your immediate commands. "Stop!" means not taking one more step forward. That one word may keep them from being hit by a car or experiencing some other tragic accident. "No!" means an immediate halt to a current action. And that one word may keep them from making a decision that brings negative consequences.

However, we as parents can easily find ourselves distracted and repeat too many times to our children, "If you do that one more time, I'm going to punish you." We become broken records that fail to follow through. This generally leads to continued disobedience until we finally snap in anger toward our children. The transgression in that situation is really ours for not being clear and consistent with our children.

Another example of creating Godly household rules includes teaching our children to respect others, since God values all people deeply. Perhaps that looks more like recognizing and helping others in need rather than demanding that they use the titles "Sir" or "Ma'am" when addressing adults. Respect for others is more naturally born out of compassion rather than rules. Jesus demonstrated compassion as He walked the earth and condemned the self-righteous leaders for burdening the people with so many rules. As parents, we can model compassion. We can lovingly require that our children respect us, other adults, and their peers with both their words and actions.

Seeing our children as young, God-following proteges helps us construct beneficial household rules. And this proper perspective of our children also helps us construct fitting consequences for rules that are broken. Making the punishment "fit the crime" is just as important as creating the rule in the first place. Over-punishing small offenses can easily create bitterness and loss of hope in children. And under-punishing large offenses can easily create a sense of self-importance and entitlement. So how do we decide what punishment is appropriate for breaking our household rules? Let me answer that question with two stories.

My son Jonathon is by nature a quiet, contemplative young man, so it's not always easy to know what he's thinking. I learned early on in his young life to gently draw him out in order to hear his thoughts and know what was in his heart. And harsh punishment would only drive him back into his quiet shell.

One day, I asked him a question, and I received an answer that made me wonder if he was lying. Lying wasn't tolerated in our home because it's an unproductive, ungodly trait. I really didn't have a planned consequence because I rarely encountered lying in my kids' lives. If I had to choose a punishment for lying, I probably would have chosen something pretty severe. But to confront Jonathon with force to uncover the lie wasn't in anyone's best interest, so I quietly and immediately took the matter to prayer. As I prayed for the truth to be revealed, my heart began to break over *the breach in our relationship*, not because of the lie itself. I realized this is how God feels when we disregard His truth.

A little later in the day, I reapproached Jonathon and asked the same question I had asked him earlier. I received the same dishonest answer. Tears welled up in my eyes and began to trickle down my cheeks. Seeing my heart-broken response softened his heart, and he immediately told me the truth and asked for forgiveness. To my knowledge, he never lied to me again. Harsh punishment—in *this* situation with *this* child—would have driven Jonathon to retreat into his shell. It was my compassion—poured out through the Holy Spirit—that brought repentance and resolution.

Let's contrast that experience with Jonathon with a story about my middle child, Heather. I'm shaking my head even as I write this so many years later! Raising Heather was a seemingly never-ending test of my endurance and patience. Although there are many stories I could tell, I'll choose one particular battle we fought when she was about six years old. Keep in mind that my personality is that of a natural leader and administrator, and I have the tendency to dictate how things are going to go without a lot of flexibility for change. Heather is built exactly the same way. Do you see the problem? My own lack of maturity and Heather's growing sense of independence led us to butt heads often.

During her kindergarten year, we had established a pattern of how to prepare for school each day. I would make sure she had an outfit washed and lying at the end of her bed so she could get ready for school quickly in the morning. Our system seemed to be working well until one morning when she didn't want to wear the particular outfit I had chosen for her. The one she wanted to wear wasn't clean. I stood at her bedroom door and told her to put on what I had prepared. "NO!," she clearly spoke, with folded arms and defiance in her eyes. The fight was on! From my perspective at the time, the disagreement was an assault against my parental authority rather than a disagreement over clothing. That perspective was somewhat correct, but I suspect my pride blinded me and kept the problem from being resolved easily. The issue behind the confrontation was that Heather wanted choice in her clothing decisions, and I had failed to recognize her growing independence. But I still had to deal with her defiance.

There was no way, in my stubbornness, that she was going to win this battle. If I had to wrestle her down and put the clothes that I chose on her, I was going to do it. I think the only difference between my six-year-old daughter and me at that moment was that I was physically bigger. Not one of my proudest moments. Yes, I won the fight that day, but after that, I built into our routine in the evenings the opportunity for her to choose (within reason) what she wanted to wear to school. Our mornings went much more smoothly after that.

Although I had to discipline Heather's defiance, there was a much better way to handle the clothing issue. I certainly could have headed off the explosive conflict if I had focused on relationship more than rules. I would have seen Heather's growing need for decision-making skills and independence. And I suppose that's really the conclusion for this chapter on punishment—to value relationship over rules. Rules are important to create boundaries for growth and maturity, but outside of the context of a loving relationship, they're unproductive in the long run.

Don't neglect punishing your child for wrong behavior; just be careful to punish with an attitude of loving discipline—like our Heavenly Father.

FOCUS QUESTIONS:

1) Do you feel that you model compassion well for your children or grandchildren? Why or why not?

___

___

___

___

___

2) Think about the rules you have in place for your kids or grandkids. Do your rules consistently point toward growing your relationship?

PRAYER

Father, have mercy on me! And help me show mercy to others. Grant me wisdom as I seek to point my children and grandchildren toward You.

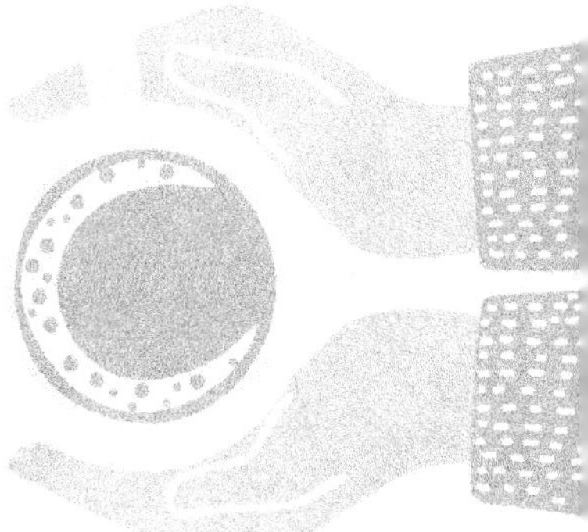

Lesson 7

Ask Questions to Unlock Creativity

Being a working mom of three growing children certainly proved challenging to my sense of "down time." It seemed like every minute was scripted, leaving very little time to play or even sit down long enough to truly listen to my children. And with my strong, dominant personality, it was easier to bark out instructions and answers than to slow down and really listen to them. But the Holy Spirit reminded me often that being present in each moment with my children was more important than I realized at the time.

I specifically remember one afternoon when I was busily putting away laundry and mentally going through the checklist of all the things that had to be accomplished before it was time to start cooking dinner. And there sat Jonathon right in the middle of the hallway with his Legos strewn out all around him. He was about eight years old at the time and was meticulously choosing and fitting together Lego pieces to create unique vehicles. Everything in me—with a large armful of folded laundry—wanted to walk right past him, stepping carefully over the Legos, so I could continue checking off my mental to-do list.

But the Holy Spirit had other plans. He whispered to my heart to put my laundry down, sit down next to Jonathon, and ask him questions about what he was building. Obediently, I brushed away enough Legos to sit cross-legged on the floor next to him. I watched him fit together several pieces and then began to ask him about the function of each vehicle he was creating. Over the next thirty minutes, he explained to me each vehicle and its function. I was amazed at his creativity. I persisted in asking questions to keep him talking. It was a rare privilege to hear what Jonathon was thinking, and I didn't want to stop the flow of creative thought and communication.

As Jonathon grew, his understanding of how things fit together continued to astound me. I would find him taking apart things and putting them back together just to find out how they work. And I remember years later walking upstairs to find electronic wires and knobs strewn out all around him right in the middle of the living room floor. I asked him what he was doing, and he replied that he was constructing an amplifier. I smiled as I remembered that eight-year-old boy fitting those little Lego pieces together. I'm humbled as I now contemplate how easily I could have walked past him that day so many years ago and not let him verbalize his emerging creativity. And I suspect the validation he experienced that day from Mom was far more important than I realized.

These days Jonathon works for an audio-visual company that designs sound and lighting systems for large auditoriums, installs them, and trains other people to use them. He is creative in ways my mind does not work. But that's the beauty of unlocking creativity in others—we don't have to think like they do; we just need to ask the right questions to draw their creativity out.

The art of asking good questions serves us well in communicating with others in every area of our lives, and it's particularly useful with our children and grandchildren. There is a God-given inclination for these young ones to seek us out for guidance, but instead of handing out answers, perhaps we would benefit them more by asking strategic questions. My children asked all kinds of questions as they were growing up. Sometimes I answered them directly, and other times I simply responded with a question of my own or directed them to a resource where they could discover their own answers.

> *The art of asking good questions serves us well in communicating with others in every area of our lives, and it's particularly useful with our children and grandchildren.*

Faith was one of the trickier topics of discussion. When they were young, I answered their questions directly, but as they got older, I wanted them to own their faith in Christ rather than believe because the people around them had given them all the correct answers. So during their teenage years, as they would come to me with dilemmas about dealing with certain situations, I tried to give them a story they could read in the Word of God that would give them guidance. And I encouraged them to ask the Holy Spirit to speak to their hearts as they read the passage of Scripture.

Sometimes they would come back to me after spending time reading and listening and present to me their answer from an "aha moment." And other times they would ask me to help them mentally and spiritually connect the dots, so to speak, and I would keep asking them questions until they reasoned their way to a good conclusion. But either way, they were searching for and finding answers rather than being told how they should think.

Now, as adults, they know the process: when a question arises, go to God's Word, and listen for the leading of the Holy Spirit. And these days, when they call, my job is to continue to ask them questions to draw out their thoughts and reasoning processes. The key to asking my kids good questions is to *know* my kids—to truly know them.

There is a passage in the Bible that I've always found interesting as well as a bit challenging. The passage is in Isaiah, and it's about a farmer who knows how to plant, harvest, and process each crop according to its uniqueness. In the story, the farmer—instructed by God—knows exactly what tools to use to produce a good harvest. Let's read Isaiah 28:26-29 (NLT) together:

> *The farmer knows just what to do, for God has given him understanding. A heavy sledge is never used to thresh black cumin; rather, it is beaten with a light stick. A threshing wheel is never rolled on cumin; instead, it is beaten lightly with a flail. Grain for bread is easily crushed, so he doesn't keep on pounding it. He threshes it under the wheels of a cart but he doesn't pulverize it. The Lord of Heaven's Armies is a wonderful teacher, and he gives the farmer great wisdom.*

I want to draw a parallel between the way a farmer uses his God-given understanding to process his crops and the way a parent uses his or her God-given understanding to raise each child.

Our children were created by God with personalities and giftings unique to His purposes for their lives. And although we all need to have the rough edges of our personalities sanded down a bit, we do well as parents to work carefully with our children's God-given personalities. For example, our daughter Kirsten is a people-person and very empathetic. It didn't take a heavy hand of punishment for her to sense the need for course-correction in her life. I simply needed to speak a gentle word of correction, and she would make the adjustment. Our daughter Heather needed firmer correction than Kirsten. Heather would take a gentle word as a mere suggestion, so I had to be very direct and authoritative in my dealing with her misbehavior. However, once administered, I was quick to follow-up by reminding her how much I love her. And with Jonathon, just a glance that conveyed the words, "Son, stop doing that," was often enough to correct his behavior.

It is critical that we, as parents, don't overcorrect our sensitive children or undercorrect our more headstrong children. The Holy Spirit is our wonderful teacher if we will allow Him to be. If we let Him guide us both in discipline and in our conversations with our kids, He will help us unlock creativity unique to each of our children. This creativity can be a powerful tool in God's Kingdom.

FOCUS QUESTIONS:

1) Take a moment to think about each of your children or grandchildren. How are they uniquely creative? How can you encourage their individual creativity?

____

____

____

____

____

____

2) Do you spend intentional time with the Holy Spirit in order to hear His direction for how to lead and correct? If not, how can you intentionally quiet yourself to hear Him?

PRAYER

Father, grant me wisdom and insight to see how my children and grandchildren have been gifted by you. And please give me creativity as I help them grow in their giftings.

Lesson 8

Deliberately Create Margin in Your Day

After reading about my experiences in Lesson 7, you may be thinking that the title "Deliberately Create Margin in Your Day" sounds a little hypocritical. After all, my days were so tightly packed that I hardly had time to listen closely to my own children. But it was specifically because of the tension in those days of raising my young ones that I learned the value of creating margin.

Rushing from place to place or task to task causes us to run right past the most important people in our lives. It prevents us from seeing divine opportunities. We've all walked past someone who could have used our help. That help might simply have been in the form of a genuine smile or an encouraging word. But perhaps we were so focused on the next task that we missed the opportunity. Creating margin means we rid our schedules of unessential busyness to leave room for more important things like spontaneous conversations, unexpected visits, and cuddles with our little ones. A less-hurried life is actually a more effective life. Yes, it's true. In a less-hurried life, we may not check as many items off our to-do lists, but we make greater impact among the people God has called us to influence most.

I wish I could say I've become an expert at creating margin, but just when I think I've mastered it, I fall back into being too busy. And the cycle of trying to bring margin back into my days begins again. Especially in the western world, many of us place value on rushing from task to task—equating our busyness to our importance. But that is a false sense of importance and one we need to replace with intentional relational connection, which is often found in the less-hurried moments in life.

What I have come to realize is that our schedules require a constant realignment to our values. We have the tendency to allow some areas of our lives to overrun others and create conflict with what is most important to us—our values. And that word—values—brings us to the heart of the issue of creating margin in our days.

In a less-hurried life, we may not check as many items off our to-do lists, but we make greater impact among the people God has called us to influence most.

It is so easy to spend our lives taking care of whatever event, task, or voice that screams loudest each day, but the most obvious needs aren't always the most important. Take a moment to ask yourself what you value most in life. This important task will help you realign your daily activities to give priority where it's needed most.

If we say our faith is most important, are we making time to be in the Lord's presence and read His Word? If our marriage is a high priority, are we making time to spend with our spouse? And if we say our relationships with our children are paramount, then are we creating space for them in our daily routines? We tend to deem most important the activities that produce money, recognition, or at least a sense of fulfillment, but these are temporal things that should not inordinately consume our time. Our most important relationships don't usually produce money or acclaim and are often not momentarily fulfilling. But those important relationships are truly our greatest treasures.

Our relationship with Christ should certainly be our highest priority, and the apostle Paul reminds us that we find our most valuable treasures in Him:

"In him (Christ) lie hidden all the treasures of wisdom and knowledge" (Colossians 2:3, NLT).

If we truly believe that *"all the treasures of wisdom and knowledge"* are hidden in Christ, shouldn't we be spending time pursuing Him and discovering all the valuable gifts He has for us?

And if children and grandchildren are a beautiful gift from God, shouldn't we be spending time with them? In the Scriptures, we're reminded that *"Children are a gift from the Lord; they are a reward from Him. Children born to a young man are like arrows in a warrior's hands"* (Psalm 127:3-4, NLT).

How we spend our time reveals our true values. Will we pursue what we value most?

My mom had a wonderful practice during my growing up years that impacts me still today. Each day when I would come home from school, Mom was sitting at the kitchen table with a bowl of popcorn and iced tea. Sometimes there were even brownies! In my younger years, I would walk in the door, drop my books on the couch, and join Mom at the table. Handfuls of popcorn later, I had vividly shared with her all the events of my day.

As I grew into my teenage years, there would be days that my adolescent moodiness silenced the table conversation. But even still, Mom's presence was enormously comforting. Years later, she shared with me that she considered those two hours surrounding my arrival home from school each day the most important hours of her day. It wasn't because I was the center of her emotional world; it was because she valued me enough to set aside time to be available to me.

Mom shared with me that she wanted to be the first one to hear the events of my day and give me the opportunity to talk through my joys, frustrations, and concerns. And she was able to look into my eyes and know the state of my heart.

Just like my mom was present each day to listen to me, I intentionally made myself fully available to my children during their younger years. As they grew into their teens, they stayed busy with school, homework, sports, music, church activities, and part-time jobs. Quality time with them became a rarity—more because of their schedules and less because of mine. But I could see that by moving a couple of items on my own calendar, I could be home at some of the same times they were at home. Although we weren't always in the same room at the same time, my presence was an important reminder to them that I valued them. And we had some good conversations along the way because I had made myself available to them.

How we spend our time reveals our true values.

One of my most consistent habits through the years has been sitting at the kitchen table each morning to read the Word of God while I eat my breakfast. As the kids were growing up, my morning ritual was normally a quiet time alone for me, but occasionally one of the kids would slide into a seat at the table and begin talking about something on their mind.

Often, those early-morning dialogs turned into important moments of growth and insight for my children. Such treasured conversation was only possible because I intentionally created margin in my mornings. My kids could approach me because they knew where to find me, and they knew I would patiently listen. Kirsten, my oldest, told me this:

> *Seeing you at the kitchen table every morning eating breakfast and reading the Bible was so comforting for me. I never wondered when I could find time to speak to you about something on my mind -- I knew I could simply meet you at the table any given morning, and you'd be there. I joined you there to chat, to process, and just to be around you. It was peaceful. I learned so much about God's character and the Bible when you shared about what you were reading, and it made me feel valued. It felt special to know that you thought I was important enough to hear about your walk with God! Most importantly, though, it modeled for me how to spend time with God and in the Word. Even now, in my own home, my Bible reading time is most often spent at my kitchen table over breakfast. I'm so thankful to have those memories with you.*

These days, I intentionally spend time playing with my grandchildren. In these early years, we are bonding by playing and spending time together. I probably say, "I love you," more often than necessary, but those words easily tumble out of my mouth when I look into their eyes. I want them to know I'm available to them. I'm preparing now for those table conversations with Mimi later. They know they're loved, and they'll know where to find me.

FOCUS QUESTIONS:

1) What do you value most in life? Take a moment to list your top five priorities in order.

2) Do you create time for each of these priorities? How can you create more margin in your day?

PRAYER

Father, please teach me to slow down enough to see the needs of those around me. And help me be willing to invest myself in the lives of others.

Lesson 9

Be Consistent and Flexible

Consistency and flexibility are two crucial parental attributes in raising stable children. And implementing consistency and flexibility is not as difficult as one might think. Being consistent with my children can be as simple as doing my devotions at the kitchen table each morning, like I mentioned in the last lesson. However, being consistent with them can also be as simple as keeping my word over and over again. Children will build their sense of truth on your ability to be consistent. And they will develop their understanding of mercy based on your flexibility. Let me explain.

Truth is like an anchor that keeps a ship from drifting away. No matter which way the wind blows or how much the sea rolls, the anchor holds the ship steady. Your children will be subject to some gale force winds of difficulty as they're growing up, and the unsteady movement of others around them can cause a lot of confusion. But if they experience dependable responses and consistent actions from you, they learn that the anchor of truth will hold them steady regardless of what others around them are doing. And as believers in Jesus Christ, the truths found in the Word of God must be our foundation for raising anchored kids.

Truth is firm and steadfast, but not necessarily rigid and legalistic. Flexibility is needed in raising children—not in compromising values, but rather in allowing for mistakes and missteps that require realignment with truth.

In one of the previous lessons, I described how differently each of my children responded to my correction. I remained consistent in holding my children to the standard (truth) that was set before them, but how I delivered correction (realignment) was often tailored to the individual child.

If we're inconsistent with our discipline or with our own integrity, our children will come to believe that truth is relative—ever-changing depending on the situation.

I vividly remember an episode with my girls in a department store that makes the point of consistency and flexibility. At the time of the incident, Kirsten and Heather were about four years old and three years old, respectively. Jonathon hadn't made his entrance into the family just yet. There was a particular department store that sold cute little girls' clothes, and I enjoyed taking Kirsten and Heather there to buy an occasional new outfit. Honestly, Kirsten was the only child truly benefitting from the shopping trip because Heather was more interested in playing hide and seek in the clothing racks.

The consistent rule when I took my children shopping was that they had to stay near me. I didn't have any reason to believe this particular shopping trip would challenge that rule. So as I was talking with Kirsten about a cute outfit, Heather wandered away. That girl was quick! Suddenly I realized she wasn't within arm's reach, and as I called out for her, there was silence. Salesclerks rushed to me to verify my child was indeed missing and promptly locked down the store. To the credit of the store personnel, they had secured the area within about thirty seconds. I was trying to remain calm on the outside, but on the inside, I was panicking. We frantically combed the store for Heather. And then, all the sudden, she popped out from a round clothing rack and yelled, "Hi!" with a smile on her face.

Of course, I was relieved we found her and that she was unharmed. I have to admit that I was also embarrassed because of the number of people who had to be involved in my child's disobedient actions. However, Heather was only three years old, and the whole episode was definitely a teachable moment. After I recovered from my own emotional overload, I reminded Heather that she had broken Mommy's rule of staying near, and I implemented the consequence of her choice to disobey. (In addition, for a few weeks after the department store episode, Heather was required to ride in the stroller so she couldn't repeat the offense!)

I laugh as I think about it all again because I suspect that Kirsten surveyed the whole situation and determined never to stray, without me even having to remind her. Kirsten learned by watching and listening; Heather learned by doing and experiencing the consequences. Each child is so different, and raising each one requires flexibility while consistently holding firm to the standard of truth.

We live in a time when people are constantly trying to redefine truth to fit their lifestyles, and it's critical that we declare the truth of the Word of God in our families and live that truth consistently in front of them. If we're inconsistent with our discipline or with our own integrity, our children will come to believe that truth is relative—ever-changing depending on the situation. So our consistency is important to the development of truth in their lives.

In addition to consistency, flexibility is crucial. Flexibility reminds us that truth is based in love, not rules.

The apostle Paul reminds us that we should "*...speak the truth in love, growing in every way more and more like Christ, who is the head of his body, the church*" (Ephesians 4:15, NLT). Our consistency supports the necessity of truth in our children's lives, and our flexibility focuses on loving them as individuals.

Many years ago, as my three young children were approaching school age, my husband and I prayed about how we should educate our children. We listened to the advice of our friends who were advocates for putting children in public schools, but we did not feel that their reasoning fit our family's desires. I was an educator and had taught in the public school system, so I knew we were making an informed decision.

I felt a strong conviction that we were to raise our children in an environment where God was welcome, not excluded. So, for us, that narrowed our decision to either homeschooling or private Christian schooling. We listened to proponents of homeschooling and felt drawn to the idea, but perhaps for a later time. Our hearts leaned toward putting our children in private Christian education, but it was—and still is!—expensive.

As we continued to pray, God began to provide the resources we needed to put our oldest child in a wonderful Christian school. And I don't want to miss the opportunity to share the backstory to this beautiful provision.

When Kirsten was a newborn, we had the opportunity to support the Christian education needs of a child in Nicaragua—the son of a pastor. The monthly commitment was not a large sum of money, but we had so little money that it was actually a sacrificial gift on our part. I knew that one day I would want to put my children in Christian education, so this was my opportunity to sow seeds now for a harvest I would reap later. We faithfully gave each month for that little boy named Ivan to graduate with a Christian education in Nicaragua. And along the way, God provided beautifully for our children to also graduate with a Christian education.

Through the years of our children's education, we went back and forth between private Christian schools and homeschooling, depending on financial ability at the time. And, for eight years, I taught at the private school where our daughters graduated as valedictorians. I opted to resign my position and return home as our youngest child, Jonathon, completed his junior year of high school. He came to me and requested that I allow him to homeschool his senior year. I questioned his motives, but he reassured me that he would use the freedom responsibly! He did. When he wasn't studying or taking homeschool cooperative learning classes, Jonathon gave his time to our church, serving the staff and learning the audio-visual side of weekend services in our large congregation. And I took that year as an opportunity to invest in my son. We worked through John Maxwell leadership studies together and enjoyed the true gift of a close, open relationship.

Consistency on my part meant adhering to the conviction of raising my children in an environment where God was welcome. Flexibility meant being willing to homeschool when needed and at other times work as a teacher to provide a way for them to attend private school. Each family is different, and parents must make educational decisions for their children based on their own convictions. However, consistency and flexibility are important no matter what decisions your family makes. Be consistent imparting your values to your children; stand on the truth of the Word of

God. And be flexible as you show your children patience and mercy, which flow from the love of Christ. Your kids will benefit.

FOCUS QUESTIONS:

1) Are you consistent in your personal life? Do your children see consistency in your words and actions?

2) Do you struggle more with consistency or flexibility? Pray about the area you're struggling in and ask God to help you grow!

PRAYER

Father help me be consistent in my pursuit of Your Word and Your righteousness. And help me be flexible in ways that model Your mercy.

Lesson 10

Institute Quiet Time

Life seems to be so much more complicated than when we were young. The days of carefree play and quiet family nights unfortunately appear to be a thing of the past. The busyness of life has crept into every aspect of our homes—from continual internet access and social media usage to involvement in a myriad of activities. But busyness isn't the only distraction that has made life seem so complicated; societal fear and personal anxiety are at an all-time high, which rob people of peace, joy, and the ability to be truly present within relationships. So how do we rescue our families from all of this chaos?

There is only one place to find true peace and joy—in the presence of God. Spending time there ourselves is of utmost importance because we lead our children by example. So, spending quality time with the Lord ourselves is our first step. But the purpose of this lesson is to create in our children a hunger for God's Word and God's presence. That is only accomplished by teaching them how to sit quietly before the Lord.

It would be so much easier if God's presence were available like a fast food drive-thru. You could just get in line, pull up to the window, transact with God, and go about your day. The problem with fast food is that it fills you up for the moment, but it's ultimately not healthy eating. So, we *could* get our time with God on the run, but before too long, we'd find ourselves spiritually malnourished and unhealthy.

There is only one place to find true peace and joy—in the presence of God.

In a world that is constantly "on the go," training our children to sit before the Lord requires intentionality. When my children were very young, I instituted what I called *quiet time*. I would require my children to go to their rooms and do a quiet activity for a prescribed amount of time. The amount of time was relative to their ages and ability to be apart from my direct oversight. I defined for them what qualified as a quiet activity: "read" a book, draw, nap, or work on a puzzle. They were welcome to sing to themselves, but electronics and talking to one another were off limits. Yes, this was challenging when the kids were under the age of four! But they adapted quickly, and after a short period of time, they seemed to look forward to their quiet time.

In my children's lives, there have been many long-term benefits to instituting quiet time. And before I talk about those long-term benefits, I'm first to admit that one short-term benefit was my sanity! I needed a few minutes each day to myself to think and study, so quiet time for my children certainly proved beneficial to my mental health as a mom.

One of the most practical long-term benefits for my kids was that they learned how to quietly entertain themselves. A child who is dependent on another person or electronics to entertain them grows into an adult who is dependent on others and electronics to entertain them. And "entertaining" subject matter for adults—particularly on electronics—can quickly get into dangerous territory. So, training our children to find appropriate ways to entertain themselves is really a life lesson that will serve them well.

> *Children are very open to God's voice, and a quiet atmosphere facilitates that opportunity.*

Facilitating a quiet atmosphere for our children brings the opportunity to learn to hear God's voice. I watch so many people today constantly filling their minds with something—anything—to override silence and solus. It's as if they don't know how to comfortably *be* with themselves or with God. As believers, it's critical that we learn to hear the voice of the Holy Spirit for comfort and direction. And learning to be comfortable in quietness is the first step. Adults who are uncomfortable being with themselves or with God will find other ways to satiate the hungry void inside them, and most of those ways easily become addictions that are difficult to break. Children are very open to God's voice, and a quiet atmosphere facilitates that opportunity.

My two-year-old granddaughter Joanna is learning to play quietly by herself because my daughter Heather wants to make sure she has plenty of opportunity to develop satisfaction in quiet solitude. And my five-month-old granddaughter Tia has a momma who is very aware that creativity in children is closely tied to quiet time. My daughter Kirsten has held off introducing Tia to flashy music, videos, and toys in order to encourage quiet, creative play.

As a writer and communicator, I certainly agree that fostering creativity begins with cultivating silence. When the noise is silenced, I can create with words. When the noise level rises in my life, I am easily distracted and unable to focus on creating messages of hope and instruction for others. Children experience the same intentional need for quiet space to foster creativity. I mentioned my son's love for Lego-building in an earlier lesson. Jonathon would sit for hours in the carpeted hallway quietly creating vehicles of all sorts. His imagination was fully engaged during those hours of play. Jonathon also loved to be outside, where he would play imaginatively by himself or with others. Quiet time looks different for every person, but it's crucial for all children (and adults!).

As a grandmother, I intentionally create quiet, interesting spaces for my grandchildren—invitations to imaginative play. Recently, my husband and I spent a few months in an apartment while our new home was under construction. I lamented over moving into the apartment because I was concerned the grandchildren wouldn't have space to play. With a bit of creativity, we arranged our space to include a corner play-kitchen, a well-lit toy closet, and easily accessible places for books and drawing tools. And, thankfully, the apartment complex had a pool, which we certainly took advantage of during the warmer months!

I probably learned how to create imaginative spaces by watching my mom do this for my children as they were growing up. I remember one house in particular where my mom and dad—Nana and Papa to my children and grandchildren—lived for a short time. At the top of the stairs, there was a small office space. And just to the right of the office space, there was a large storage closet behind a short door. Nana and Papa carpeted the storage closet and installed bright lighting. It became a perfect children's playroom which the kids absolutely loved. I also remember in that same house, Papa set up the camping tent on the large back deck so the children could "go camping" during the warmer months of the year. Those are great memories for us all, and creating them didn't require much effort.

A second long-term benefit of intentionally creating quiet times and places for my children is that they developed a love for reading. As a mom, a grandmother, a former schoolteacher, and a minister of the Gospel, I highly value encouraging children to read. The possibilities for growth are unending for those who love literature. My children's love for reading in turn facilitated a desire for reading God's Word. In this life, there is nothing more valuable than the rich treasure of God's Word.

Like many things in life, children mimic what they see. If they see you constantly on your phone scrolling Instagram or texting friends, they'll likely develop similar habits. However, if you are purposeful about reading a variety of books -- most importantly, the Bible -- in front of your kids, they'll begin to pick up books as well. Make age-appropriate, exciting books available to your children, and engage with them! My children still share with me how much they loved laying on my bed in the evenings and listening to me read *The Chronicles of Narnia* by C.S. Lewis out loud, chapter by chapter.

Quiet creativity and a love for reading will be an asset to your children for the rest of their lives. While they're young, be intentional about creating quiet time for your children each day. You will see them mature in so many beautiful ways from your purposeful investment.

FOCUS QUESTIONS:

1) As a child, what types of creative activities did you enjoy? Can you introduce those same (or similar) activities to your children or grandchildren?

____

____

____

____

2) Are you modeling quiet time for your kids? How can you intentionally embrace silence and/or being still during your day?

PRAYER

Father, help me walk in Your peace. Remind me to live from the position of Your peace.

Lesson 11

Make Them Work for It

As adults, many of us have developed a good understanding of the value of work. We work for wages. We work to add value to a company or group of people. We work with a sense of purpose. God says work is good. For us as adults, those are all good reasons to work. And establishing beneficial work habits in our children and grandchildren is essential to their development.

Please don't misunderstand me—I'm not speaking about child labor! I support children learning the *value* of work. And children's work begins with play. A child's fine motor and gross motor skills are developed beginning even as early as one month old. My daughter Heather and I took her children Joanna (grandchild number one—two years old) and Joshua (grandchild number three—seven weeks old) to the trampoline park to play. Joanna loves to jump, so the trampoline park is a wonderful indoor activity to exhaust all of that two-year-old energy! Little Joshua is just old enough to watch his big sister, and he desperately wants to do what she does.

I took off Joshua's socks so his feet could feel the trampoline. I let him touch one of the foam balls Joanna was playing with. His excitement caused his arms and legs to start flailing, and I had to uncurl his fingers so he could feel the ball. His desire to participate in all the fun was evident even at seven weeks old—and for him, learning how to use his arms and legs is work!

Teaching Joanna the value of work at two years old is as simple as asking her to bring Joshua the ball or to hold his bottle while Mommy takes him out of the stroller. Allowing Joanna to help unload the dishwasher—which she absolutely loves to do—is her work. Singing a song with her while we pick up toys together in her room is also a playful way to learn the value of work. As Joanna cooperates with putting her toys away, we're generous with our words of encouragement towards her.

Joanna is naturally adept at many gross motor activities. Her daddy enjoys participating in Spartan races, and he often takes Joanna with him to the ROTC obstacle course at the local high school. He helps her climb, jump, and maneuver through the obstacles that are her size. Joanna is gaining strength while she's having fun with her daddy. She's learning the value of working hard to discipline her body without realizing she's gaining such valuable skills. And again, Joanna receives words of encouragement as she exerts effort on each obstacle.

My daughter Kirsten's little girl Tia (grandchild number two—six months old) helps her mommy turn off the lights by pushing down the light switch on the wall. It may sound simple, but learning the joy of a job done well can start in infancy. Tia also enjoys knocking down anything that has been stacked up. When we stack blocks or toys, she'll joyfully and enthusiastically push them over. (I remember Joanna doing this as well, but now she is old enough to stack them up herself before knocking them down!)

As children get older, the time will come to start requiring them to help with household chores, whether or not they consider the tasks enjoyable. Part of living together as a family is learning to be a responsible member of the team. And our children gain important skills and a sense of belonging by being a valued part of the team. It's easy as adults to slip into the habit of doing all the chores ourselves—or hiring them out—because it takes more time to train our children to complete the tasks properly than to complete them ourselves. But these team-building skills of household chores are extremely important lessons for our children and are part of our responsibility to teach.

The goal is to develop in our children a sense of purpose as well as the self-discipline necessary to pursue that purpose.

With toddlers, start with something simple, such as carrying folded kitchen towels to the kitchen and putting them away. As they get older, teach them to fold the clean laundry and deliver the items to the proper rooms. By the time they're in their early teens, they'll be sorting, washing, folding, and delivering without oversight. This, of course, applies to many other areas of home upkeep, inside and outside. But this is a progression that requires intentionality at every stage of implementation.

As we teach our children the value of work, the end goal is not simply to teach them how to do chores or to earn a living. Really, the goal is to develop in our children a sense of purpose as well as the self-discipline necessary to pursue that purpose. As Jesus was preparing to go to the cross, He prayed to His Father, *"I brought glory to you here on earth by completing the work you gave me to do"* (John 17:4, NLT). Some of Jesus' work on earth was physical work, and some was relational. Some of the work was simply being a vessel available for His Father's use. Jesus' life was one of sacrificial investment in the lives of others. The apostle Peter reminds us of this: *"For God called you to do good, even if it means suffering, just as Christ suffered for you. He is your example, and you must follow in his steps"* (1 Peter 2:21, NLT).

As we're teaching our children the value of a job well done, we're also teaching them to generously give of themselves for the good of those around them. So, not all their work should be compensated with allowance or privilege. Part of their work-training should involve volunteering their time with no tangible return for their effort. If we're not careful, we easily attach monetary value to our work and devalue the importance of volunteering. Giving our time and service without compensation should be just as valuable as earning money in exchange for our labor. There are many opportunities available in our communities for family volunteer work; you simply need to seek it out.

For example, as my children moved into their young adult years, they began volunteering with the Bridge Ministry in Nashville, serving individuals who are homeless and under-resourced. Their experience volunteering in that ministry was so impactful that it influenced me to get involved as well. Throughout the next seven years, at least one of us was present to volunteer our time in the ministry on Tuesday evenings. And as a really great bonus from the time we spent volunteering, my daughter Kirsten met her husband there, who was volunteering as well!

So, how do we cultivate a balanced view of work—both paid and volunteer—in our children? The answer is simple: by creating a culture of generosity in our homes. The Bible teaches us that the love of money is the root of all evil. That's a bold statement—one that should arrest our attention. If the love of money is that powerful, then we need to intentionally practice the opposite action, which is deliberate generosity. Generosity is not focused solely on money. The giving of our money is one mark of generosity, but being generous is an act of the heart and involves our time and talent as well as our money.

God is generous; therefore, we should also be generous. To be generous is to give wisely without concern that we will have enough for ourselves. Our responsibility is to model this heart of generosity for our children. That means we must cultivate generosity in our own hearts first. God modeled this for us when He sent His Son Jesus Christ to die on the cross in our place, giving us a way to have a relationship with Himself through Christ's sacrifice and resurrection. *"For this is how God loved the world: He gave his one and only Son, so that everyone who believes in him will not perish but have eternal life"* (John 3:16, NLT). God gave what was precious to Him for our benefit. He gave generously. We must not hold on too tightly to anything in this life—including money.

Although we want to be cautious not to "spoil" our children, teaching them the value of work—including volunteer work—should be taught in tandem with being generous toward our children. From us, they should learn that work is sometimes exchanged for money and sometimes simply for the honor of serving others. And from us, they should also learn that parents enjoy giving to their children.

My husband and I tried to create this "giving/requiring work" balance with our children as they approached their sixteenth birthdays. The excitement of getting their driver's licenses would have been greatly tempered if they had no car to drive. And honestly, by that time, I was ready for them to get themselves to all their activities. I was truly feeling like a chauffeur! So, we were committed to making sure they each had a car to drive when they turned sixteen. Each family has to approach teenage car ownership according to what works best for them, but let me explain our method. Perhaps you'll be inspired by our process.

As the kids approached their twelfth birthdays, we began encouraging them to find ways to earn money. We opened a joint savings account with each of them where they could place their earnings. The prospect of purchasing a car when they turned sixteen provided the motivation they needed to earn money. We had three rules about their earnings: 1) Earning money can't interfere with your schoolwork; 2) Earning money can't interfere with church activities; 3) Money earned had to be tithed. So, between the ages of approximately twelve and sixteen years old, they worked hard to build their savings accounts.

When Kirsten (our oldest child) turned fifteen and began student-driving, my husband and I purchased a late-model four-door sedan for each of the kids to drive when they turned sixteen. Driving the "family" vehicle gave her unhindered access to employment until the next child came of age and needed the car. When Kirsten was ready to buy her first car, we matched her money saved to help her make a good purchase. We did the same for Heather (our second child). Please notice how we, as parents, gave in ways that assisted them to reach their goals. We did not simply hand them a car with no effort on their part, but we were careful not to be so stingy with them that they despaired in frustration.

Our plan worked well with child number one and child number two. But I still remember the day that our son Jonathon (child number three) sat down in the driver's seat of our "family" vehicle. Nearing his sixteenth birthday, he was well on his way to exceeding six feet in height. He slid into the driver's seat and pushed the seat back as far as it would go. Still, his knees hit the steering wheel, and his head hit the ceiling. We obviously had to scramble to make a different car decision for Jonathon! Yes, he had saved some money and done his part, but he still had a couple of money-earning years ahead of him before he could afford to purchase a car even with our "matching" money. My dad came to the rescue and offered Jonathon a truck he had been driving for years (and my grandfather drove it for a couple of years before that). We were all overjoyed at my father's generosity. And Jonathon never took Papa's gift for granted. He drove that truck for years until he was ready to purchase his own vehicle (with no matching funds needed from us).

Generosity begets generosity. So, yes, make your children work for what they want. But don't hesitate to come alongside them to help them reach their goals. God does the same for us!

FOCUS QUESTIONS:

1) What was your first job as a teenager or adult? Do you feel that the skills you learned at home helped you succeed in your first job? Why or why not?

2) What have your children and grandchildren learned about generosity through your life? Do you give freely to others, or do you hold tightly to your income or possessions? How can you increase your own generosity so that your kids can see the benefit of giving to others?

____

____

____

____

____

____

PRAYER

Father, teach me gratitude. Train me to live with an open hand toward You and others. Remind me that You are my provision.

Lesson 12

Pray

Even though this lesson on prayer is nestled in the last half of this book, it's important to emphasize that prayer is truly the foundation of every part of the Christian life. I'm not talking about the list of things we routinely ask God for, although He doesn't mind us asking. And I'm not talking about attempting to get God to see from our point of view, which is futile. I'm talking about cultivating a relationship with the only One who truly knows us; in His divine wisdom, He carefully crafted each of us to be born at just the right time.

Our children were not given to us by God to fulfill our own hopes and dreams. They were given to us as a gift of love that we are to return to God by raising them to impact this world for His Kingdom. We, as well as our children and grandchildren, are positioned to shift culture. With such a lofty purpose, what could possibly be more important than intentionally spending time with the only One who has the blueprints for our lives?

Prayer is an ongoing conversation between the God of the universe and His creation. With the Holy Spirit living inside us, attuning our spirits to

His voice becomes our mode of living a life of faith. If we're not careful, we will neglect to listen attentively to the voice of the Holy Spirit and instead listen to the voice of culture. But God has called us to shift culture, not conform to it.

> *Prayer is an ongoing conversation between the God of the universe and His creation.*

Teaching our children to pray by *being* a person of prayer is one of the most important lessons we can teach our children. One of the most impressionable memories I have of my father when I was about eighteen years old is him kneeling beside his bed in morning prayer. I, too, have knelt in prayer at my bedside since before I can remember. I suppose I subconsciously learned that habitual practice from watching my dad during my growing up years. For some reason, it just didn't make a conscious impression on me until I was a young adult.

I knew my mother too was a woman of prayer, not because I consistently heard or saw her praying, but because her relationship with Jesus was so authentic and vibrant that she obviously spent time with Him. My objective in raising my own children was always to stay so close to Jesus that they too would want to know Him personally and intimately.

I am painfully aware that there are many moms, dads, grandmas, and grandpas reading this book who don't have ongoing access to their children/grandchildren. I have volunteered in a women's prison, where I was pained to discover there are mommas who might—if they're lucky—get to see and touch their children only occasionally. And I have many friends outside prison walls who rarely get to see their children or grandchildren because of geographical or relational distance. I know it's painful.

But the beautiful thing about prayer is that it has no constraints of distance or access. You can pray for your child or grandchild whether you are physically present with them or whether they are even aware of your prayers. I try to remind my friends in prison that they are positioned to be incredibly effective in their children's and grandchildren's lives through prayer. Prayer may be the only method they have of influencing their children and grandchildren, but it is in fact the MOST important influence.

Our personal sensitivity to the Holy Spirit is crucial in effective prayer. If we are distracted or consumed with our own lives, we will miss critical opportunities to pray for those we love. Praying in tongues is unequivocally the most effective method to pray when you don't know what to ask for. There have been many times—day and night—when I instinctively knew I needed to pray for my family but had no idea what I needed to pray about. Had I not been well-acquainted with praying in tongues, I would have struggled for words. But praying in tongues gives me the ability to pray with boldness even when I have no idea what I am praying about. If you have not yet been filled with the power of the Holy Spirit with the evidence of speaking in tongues, you are missing a crucial part of effective prayer.

When we pray in our native tongues—mine is English—we would do well to pray the Word of God over our children and grandchildren. Two of my favorite passages to pray over my family are Psalm 91 and Ephesians 3:14-21. Both of those passages speak of the nearness of God to us. His presence is our lifeline to maneuvering through this life, and I desperately want my children and grandchildren to stay close to Him. Both passages also speak of power, protection, anointing, and purpose, which are crucial to living boldly for Christ.

I remember when my daughter Kirsten attended college eight hours away from our home. She was close enough that I could drive to the college, but far enough away that I couldn't get to her quickly. So, I prayed—a lot. She is a trustworthy woman, and she was then as well, so my prayers were not as much about keeping her out of trouble as they were about protecting her life. Although my prayers weren't borne out of paranoia, I deliberately prayed Psalm 91 over her (as well as over our daughter Heather and our son Jonathon).

I got a phone call from Kirsten one morning to inform me of an incident that had happened a couple of nights prior to her call. She said she and her friends were headed back to campus after a late-night movie. It was an icy winter evening, and their car slid on the ice and spun around on the highway ramp, leaving the car headed the wrong direction on the narrow ramp. Kirsten was in the front passenger seat. As the car was sliding, Kirsten said she could see that her side of the car was about to collide with the concrete wall. Kirsten said everything felt like it was in slow motion, but she remembers a picture flashing through her mind of four angels surrounding the car, preventing them from hitting the barrier. "*For he will order his angels to protect you wherever you go. They will hold you up with their hands so you won't even hurt your foot on a stone*" (Psalm 91:11-12, NLT). Or in Kirsten's experience, "they will hold you up with their hands so you don't collide with the concrete wall." Praise God!

I had been praying Psalm 91 over her. Whether it was at the exact moment she was in peril, I don't know. But God's Word never returns void; it always accomplishes its purpose. God is the One who sees and watches over all the events of our families' lives, but He has offered us the opportunity to partner in His work through our lives by agreeing with His Word in prayer.

I was recently reading the Old Testament book of 2 Kings, and the story of Hezekiah arrested my attention. Although I've read his story many times, I saw something different this time. King Hezekiah did much good in Judah during his reign:

> *"He did what was pleasing in the Lord's sight, just as his ancestor David had done. He removed the pagan shrines, smashed the sacred pillars, and cut down the Asherah poles. He broke up the bronze serpent that Moses had made, because the people of Israel had been offering sacrifices to it. The bronze serpent was called Nehushtan. Hezekiah trusted in the Lord, the God of Israel. There was no one like him among all the kings of Judah, either before or after his time."*
> (2 Kings 18:3-5, NLT)

But, despite all the good he did, his son Manasseh and grandson Amon were two of the most despicable kings who ruled over Judah, leading the people into all kinds of sin. What happened? Although the Biblical text doesn't explain all the details of the circumstances or their family relationships, perhaps a statement made by Hezekiah a little further into the story might give us some insight.

Hezekiah had seen God rescue Judah from the threat of Assyrian invasion, and he had also personally received God's merciful gift of healing. When Hezekiah became deathly ill, he prayed fervently that God would have mercy on him. And God granted him fifteen more years. It was during those fifteen years that his son Manasseh was born. Through the Biblical text, we see evidence that Hezekiah may have succumbed to his own pride during those fifteen years. And the prophet Isaiah told him that Babylon would conquer Judah and that some of Manasseh's descendants would be taken away into exile (see 2 Kings 20:12-18).

> *"Then Hezekiah said to Isaiah, 'This message you have given me from the Lord is good.' For the king was thinking, 'At least there will be peace and security during my lifetime.'"*
> (2 Kings 20:19, NLT)

In my opinion, Hezekiah missed it; he missed the opportunity to ask God to change (or even delay) the prediction upon his descendants. It was as if Hezekiah had what he wanted in the moment and neglected to focus on the generations to come. The detestable practices of his son and grandson (see 2 Kings 21) seem to offer proof of the self-focused end to Hezekiah's life.

I would encourage all of us to simply be intentional. Pray intentionally for your children and grandchildren. Pray for the generations yet to be born. Pray the Word of God over your family. Pray in the power of the Holy Spirit. Pray.

FOCUS QUESTIONS:

1) Did your own parents or grandparents model prayer? If so, what do you remember? If not, who do you know who prays faithfully?

___

___

___

___

___

2) If you're not sure how to pray for your kids, a great practice is praying Scriptures. Can you think of a verse or two to pray over your children/grandchildren?

PRAYER

Father, I come to You with a humble heart; please teach me to pray.

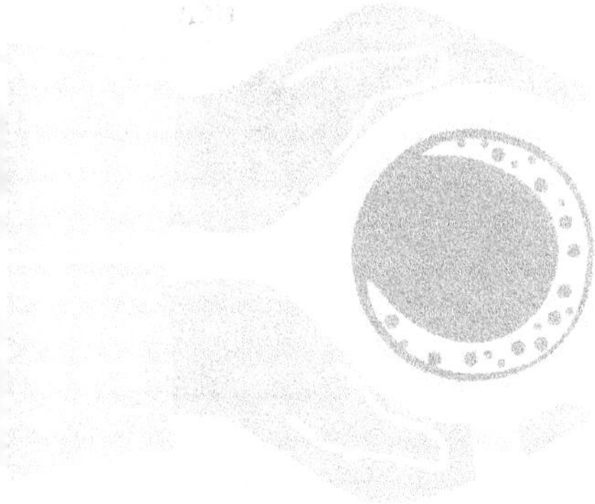

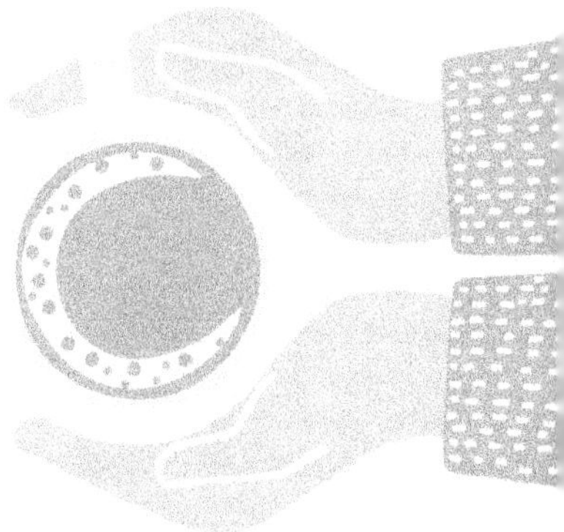

Lesson 13

Be Intentional with Words

I love words. As a writer and speaker, words are my craft. Although we certainly communicate through facial expression and actions, words are our most effective means of direct communication. And our words impact our children and grandchildren. The words we choose to speak are important. The words we choose not to speak are important. Even when our mouths are shut, the words we hear and listen to can be life-giving or life-depleting.

Some of the most negatively impactful statements in my life were made by people who didn't intentionally mean to hurt or offend me. Once, a high school teacher looked at my artistic creation—of which I was very proud—and said, "Oh, Sweetie, this [art] just isn't your cup of tea." It led me to believe for many years that I was not creative. And in my adult years, I heard a side conversation between two people I respected saying of me, "She's socially awkward," which led me to believe that I couldn't lead others with confidence, love, and compassion.

Beyond the words of our peers and acquaintances, there are many lies the enemy of our souls speaks to us. One lie he has used over and over again in my life is, "Nobody cares about you." (But now, when I hear that in my thinking, I laugh because I know it's a ploy! He's trying to distract me from the Kingdom work God has assigned to me.)

If we examine the words we've allowed to limit us, we'll begin to recognize some patterns. For example, I'm currently writing my twelfth book; that's creativity at work! God's plan for my life included creativity, and Satan attempted to squelch it. I founded a nonprofit, which requires leading with confidence, love, and compassion, and Satan tried to convince me I couldn't. And I heard him say, "Nobody cares," but I know it's simply untrue. I am surrounded by a beautiful, loving family and a wonderful church family. I have many friends for whom I care deeply and who care deeply for me. Over and over again, Satan's efforts to distract me from God's plan started with just a few words.

> *Our young ones need to be so filled with God's thoughts about them that they can easily counter any negative words spoken over them.*

Although I've certainly moved past those hurtful words, they still occasionally reverberate in my thinking, and I have to replace those negative thoughts with what God says about me.

It's crucial when we're raising children to purposefully fill their hearts and minds with what God says about them—His beloved creation. And it's critically important that we choose our words to our children very carefully. Unthinking and unwise people will insert their opinions into our children's and grandchildren's lives. Consequently, our young ones need to be so filled with God's thoughts about them that they can easily counter any negative words spoken over them.

Practically speaking, here are some statements we would do well to remind our children of:

When the world says that I am a failure, God says I am His masterpiece.

"For we are God's masterpiece. He has created us anew in Christ Jesus, so we can do the good things he planned for us long ago."
(Ephesians 2:10, NLT)

When the world disregards me, God says I am fearfully and wonderfully made.

"I praise you because I am fearfully and wonderfully made; your works are wonderful, I know that full well."
(Psalm 139:14, NIV)

When the world says I can't succeed, God says I am the head and not the tail.

"If you listen to these commands of the Lord your God that I am giving you today, and if you carefully obey them, the Lord will make you the head and not the tail, and you will always be on top and never at the bottom."
(Deuteronomy 28:13, NLT)

When the world suggests that I am forgotten, God says that I am loved.

"No power in the sky above or in the earth below—indeed, nothing in all creation will ever be able to separate us from the love of God that is revealed in Christ Jesus our Lord."
(Romans 8:39, NLT)

When the world isolates me, God says that I am not alone.

"... For God has said, 'I will never fail you. I will never abandon you.'"
(Hebrews 13:5b, NLT)

When the world says I'm incapable, God says that He is my help.

"I lift up my eyes to the mountains—where does my help come from?
My help comes from the Lord, the Maker of heaven and earth."
(Psalm 121: 1-2, NIV)

When the world says that I am a victim, God says that I'm more than a conqueror in Christ Jesus.

"No, despite all these things, overwhelming victory
is ours through Christ, who loved us."
(Romans 8:37, NLT)

When the world says I'm worthless, God says that I am clothed in the righteousness of His Son.

"But it is due to Him that you are in Christ Jesus, who became to us wisdom
from God, and righteousness and sanctification, and redemption ..."
(1 Corinthians 1:30, NASB)

When the world tries to harm me, God says that no weapon formed against me will prosper.

"'No weapon that is formed against you will succeed;
And you will condemn every tongue that accuses you in judgment.
This is the heritage of the servants of the Lord,

And their vindication is from Me,' declares the Lord."
(Isaiah 54:17, NASB)

When the world says I'm wounded, God says that I am healed.

"Heal me, O Lord, and I shall be healed;
save me, and I shall be saved,
for you are my praise."
(Jeremiah 17:14, ESV)

When the world says I'm stupid, God says that I can have the mind of Christ.

"Have this mind among yourselves, which is yours in Christ Jesus, who, though he was in the form of God, did not count equality with God a thing to be grasped, but emptied himself, by taking the form of a servant, being born in the likeness of men."
(Philippians 2:5-7, ESV)

When the world mocks me, God says that I can walk in His wisdom and discernment.

"If any of you lacks wisdom, let him ask God, who gives generously
to all without reproach, and it will be given him."
(James 1:5, ESV)

One of the most important aspects of speaking words of life is to speak from an eternal perspective. If we see our child or grandchild as a two-year-old terror or a rebellious teenager, they often conform to our opinion of them. They may be acting badly today, but part of our responsibility is to see them as the mature Christ-follower they'll be tomorrow. My daughter, Kirsten, wanted to share her experience as a recipient of words of life:

"Self-admittedly, I was a pretty awkward middle schooler. I had braces, acne, and was a little chubby. I lacked confidence and allowed myself to fade into the background at school. But my mom was my biggest support and cheerleader, no matter what. Even when she couldn't see it in my actions, she continually told me that I was a leader, and a success, and a beautiful person, inside and out. I never felt like she lied to me, even though I didn't feel like I was any of those things. I truly felt like she was telling me who I really was going to be someday, when I grew up. In those moments when I felt lost, alone, and down on myself, I needed my mom's life-giving words. What I couldn't see for myself, she called out in me. I'm so grateful, because her words are a huge part of the reason I believe in myself today."

Speak to who they are becoming. Speak to who God made them to be. And the only way we can truly do that is if we stay filled up with God ourselves. The words that spill out of our mouths come directly from our hearts. So we would do well to keep our hearts filled up with God's Word. We are also in the process of becoming who Christ called us to be, so we must extend grace to our children just as God extends it to us.

A second aspect of speaking life is knowing when *not* to speak. In a world filled with noise, our children will constantly have voices vying for their attention – but they need to know how to hear God's voice above all things. If we as parents are constantly speaking, we run the risk of bulldozing the voice of the Holy Spirit in our children's lives. When our kids are young, they require a lot of words – specific instructions, direction, and affirmation. And while that need doesn't diminish as our children grow, our kids need to begin to hear their instructions and affirmation from the Holy Spirit as well.

I vividly remember walking alongside each of my young adult children through episodes when they were unjustly discredited. As a strong mother, I wanted to get in the middle of each of those situations and let my children's accusers know just how off-base they were (in very certain terms). But the Holy Spirit reminded me that those situations were opportunities to let

God defend my children. And it was more important to allow my children to see God work on their behalf than express my disapproval of the way those situations had been handled. My mother used to say, "If you step in, you tie God's hands." I wanted my children to know the strength of their God. So, I quietly reminded my children to take their offenses to God and let Him work it out. In each situation, God eventually vindicated my children. And today, they know where their help comes from. *"My help comes from the Lord, who made heaven and earth"* (Psalm 121:2, NLT).

We must choose wisely the words we speak and the words we leave unspoken.

"Know this, my beloved brothers: let every person be quick to hear, slow to speak, slow to anger; for the anger of man does not produce the righteousness of God."
(James 1:19-20, ESV)

"Death and life are in the power of the tongue, and those who love it will eat its fruits."
(Proverbs 18:21, ESV)

FOCUS QUESTIONS:

1) What lies has the enemy told you throughout your life? Do any of the verses in this lesson stand out to you?

____

____

____

____

____

2) How can you be more intentional today about speaking life into your children or grandchildren?

PRAYER

Father, help me discern the lies of the enemy both in my own life and the lives of my loved ones. Teach me to speak the truths in Your Word to counter the enemy's tactics.

Lesson 14

Serve Together as a Family

I wish I would have embodied the principle of serving together as a family earlier in my life. My first encounter serving our community with my children didn't come until they were young adults. It's not that we didn't find opportunities to serve prior to that time; it's that we didn't serve together.

When my children were young adults, a group of their friends decided to begin serving the homeless of Nashville on Tuesday nights through an established Christian ministry. They seemed to really enjoy their experience, so I decided to join them. I gained so much from the experience that I continued to help on Tuesday nights for the next seven years.

While serving on Tuesday nights, I watched my children grow in many ways. Kirsten met her future husband, Jordan, as they both served. Heather's heart of compassion grew for others. And Jonathon joined us as he was able, bringing a sense of stability and strength in every situation. My parents even joined in the experience! After they moved to Nashville, Mom came a couple of times though she was ill, and my dad continued to serve with me even after Mom's death. Christmastime was most special of all, as my husband, my dad, and all our children were able to serve together.

During those years that we were serving the homeless, our church also began serving the community through what we called Second Saturdays. Each second Saturday of the month, our church would choose a project in the community, and we would all get to work! I loved watching families in our church serve together. Although the many families' young children were unable to significantly contribute to the work itself, they benefited greatly by working alongside their parents and participating in giving beyond themselves.

I've learned that there are many benefits to serving together as a family, including having a common purpose, learning to give sacrificially, and seeing beyond ourselves.

Having a common purpose gives us, as families, a common language. Conversations naturally develop around experiences we share. And those dialogs are often the springboard for deeper conversations.

For example, there were many times serving in compassion ministry that we encountered individuals who were confused, depressed, drunk, or high on drugs. But we also encountered people who, despite their circumstances, exuded joy and courage. In every encounter, we came away a little richer in understanding and compassion. Because we shared those experiences, our discussions centered around Christ's love in the midst of injustice and difficulty. Those kinds of conversations can certainly be eye-opening and life changing.

There was one man in particular at the homeless ministry—we'll call him Justin—who adopted our family as his own. He was older than me, probably six feet five inches tall, and obviously of a different ethnicity. So, it was rather humorous when he would bound across the serving area shouting, "Hi, Mom!" to me. His breath often smelled of alcohol, and he might not have bathed for a few days. But we wrapped our love around him the best we knew how.

The apostle Paul reminds us: "*. . . Be humble, thinking of others as better than yourselves. Don't look out only for your own interests, but take an interest in others, too*" (Philippians 2:3-4, NLT).

Although we haven't seen Justin in many months, each member of my family smiles when his name is mentioned. Justin taught us to love people who are seemingly different than us. And, really, the only difference between us is a series of choices and circumstances. Through Justin and many others, we were reminded every Tuesday night that none of us is very far away from losing everything we've worked for and everything we love. As a family, that's a precious understanding to have in common. And I think that makes us love one another just a little more deeply.

By serving as a family, we've also learned to give sacrificially. I'm not necessarily referring to money; I'm talking more about giving our time to do tasks that may not have anything to do with our giftings or education—tasks we may not have even wanted to do. And often, those tasks include getting dirty.

I remember one Saturday morning our church chose the project of landscaping a local elementary school. Our sons-in-law had shovels in hand digging large holes and planting trees. I can't say landscaping is my forte, but I can certainly dig a small hole with a hand-trowel. Both of our daughters and our son happened to be assigned to work under the same big tree with me and my husband. So, together, we were pulling weeds and planting flowers. Although the job was not especially fun, I remember laughing as we were working. Good memories were made that day serving together as a family. (And unfortunately, Kirsten and Jeff came away with more than fond memories—poison ivy was lurking under the tree!)

When we, as adults, serve others, we're training our young ones to see beyond themselves. It's easy to busy our lives with activities that focus on our own well-being. But when we take time to focus on others, it makes an impactful statement to the people around us, including our children. And I'm looking forward to the days of serving when our grandchildren are old enough to work alongside us. Choosing tasks that make room for small hands and big mistakes is an important part of parenting and grandparenting. Serving is a matter of the heart, and encouraging that giving attitude as early as possible is beneficial.

> When we, as adults, serve others, we're training our young ones to see beyond themselves.

One very accessible place to serve is in the local church. My husband and I began attending Cornerstone Nashville in 1993 when Kirsten was just one year old. Today, it's really gratifying to walk in the church doors on Sunday morning to see our children serving in different capacities. Kirsten and Jordan greet new families and help them get acclimated. Heather often serves in the children's area, and her husband Seth runs the coffee shop in our church's lobby. And although Jonathon is living in Memphis, he is also serving his local church on the production team each Sunday. My husband is a team captain for ushers, and you never know where you'll find me serving. I enjoy diversifying my serving experiences!

To echo the words of the psalmist: *"A single day in your courts is better than a thousand anywhere else! I would rather be a gatekeeper in the house of my God than live the good life in the homes of the wicked"* (Psalm 84:10, NLT). Serving in the House of the Lord is an honor and a privilege. Our children and grandchildren benefit greatly by not only watching us serve but serving right along with us.

Now that my children are grown and have homes of their own, I have discovered even greater joy in serving with them within DSM, the nonprofit organization I founded in 2017. My children passionately serve with me in the work we do in Pakistan and here in the United States, preaching the gospel and seeing lives changed. I am watching them grow yet again in compassion ministry and administrative duties. They're getting first-hand experience working with a board of directors, donors, nonprofit law, fundraisers, communication, and marketing. And they're reaching around the world loving people they've not yet met. My grandchildren are still too young to know that their sphere of influence is global. But we'll find ways to include them as they get a little older, so they'll begin taking ownership of the vision right along with us.

What opportunities are you giving your children and grandchildren to serve others alongside you? We can pass along many things to our descendants—money, land, and possessions. But what about passing along a love for others and the passion to serve them? What about walking out our faith with our children and grandchildren in very tangible ways, such as practically serving others?

James reminds us that practical service is evidence of true faith: "*What good is it, dear brothers and sisters, if you say you have faith but don't show it by your actions? Can that kind of faith save anyone? Suppose you see a brother or sister who has no food or clothing, and you say, 'Good-bye and have a good day; stay warm and eat well'—but then you don't give that person any food or clothing. What good does that do? So you see, faith by itself isn't enough. Unless it produces good deeds, it is dead and useless*" (James 2:14-17, NLT).

Let's give the people around us a practical way to see Jesus. And let's show our children and grandchildren the actions of true faith. Serve together as a family!

FOCUS QUESTIONS:

1) Serving is a selfless act! Do you think that you serve others well and often? Why or why not?

2) How can you include your children or grandchildren in serving this month?

PRAYER

Father, Your Son Jesus the ultimate example of servanthood. Help me follow in His footsteps.

Lesson 15

Create a Culture of Yes

"Mom, would you take me to the park?" asks your seven-year-old son. "No, I have some errands to run," you casually answer. Why is it so much easier for us as parents to say no than yes? We often tell our children no without putting much thought into whether we can work their request into our schedules. Would it really be that much of an imposition to stop by the park on the way to the store and let him play for twenty minutes?

When your toddler says, "Mommy . . . ?" for the fiftieth time today, it's tempting to follow each inquisition with "Not right now" or, worse yet, silence. We grow weary with the unending effort it takes to raise our young ones, and we often give negative answers or no answer at all when we could be leaning much more heavily toward a positive response. I'm not advocating giving our children whatever they want, but we need to examine the reason behind our responses. Most of the time, the difference between a negative and positive response is simply our own willingness.

Turning our no into yes may be as easy as rearranging our to-do list. But sometimes the issue of saying no too often is buried deep within us and needs to be uncovered. Have we grown impatient with our children because of our busyness or because of our selfishness? Have we lost the wonder and enjoyment of watching our children learn new things? Perhaps we've lost sight of our role in stewarding God's beautiful creation—our children. Whatever the reason for our negative response pattern, we need to regain proper perspective and shift our attitudes.

> *Creating a culture of yes in our interactions with our children begins with us: our willingness to adjust our schedules, attitudes, and behaviors and living consistent lives that our children can follow.*

As parents, we are given the responsibility to discipline and correct when needed. And there are times we certainly need to say no to our children. Situations that are detrimental to our children, purchases that are unwise, and people who are bad influences are all good reasons to say no. But are we just as quick to say yes to growth opportunities, playtime, and quality time with our children, even when it's inconvenient for us?

Making time to play is also a big part of grandparenting. Grandparenting has become one of my greatest joys in life, and I imagine that most grandparents would agree with me. My reasons for enjoying my grandchildren so much are mostly relational. I get to sow love, acceptance, and value into my grandchildren as we play together. Because my children are wonderful and attentive parents, I am able to focus more on meaningful interaction than on meeting my grandkids' most basic needs. Although I vividly remember the constant lack of sleep and the incessant attentiveness to my own children's needs as they were growing up, now I get to focus on the joys of relationship with my grandchildren while my children take care of the exhausting tasks like midnight feedings!

As a writer, speaker, CEO of a nonprofit, and volunteer at my church, I have plenty of tasks to keep me busy day to day, but my ministry and business responsibilities often come to a halt when I get a phone call from one of my daughters inviting me to come play with the grandbabies. We climb, slide, run, and swing for about an hour until the grandbabies (and Mimi) are worn out. Then they head toward home for naptime, and my work resumes.

It would be easy to say no when my daughters call to ask if I'd like to join in the fun. After all, I could reason that I'm a busy person with meaningful work to be done. But I'm finding that when I put relationships first, somehow my work still gets done. My effort—my *yes*—to be with my grandchildren is worth the time invested. Although they are very young right now, the relationships I'm building with them will serve us well for the rest of our lives.

However, our willingness to invest our time in our children and grandchildren is not the only thing that matters in creating a culture of yes. Our behavior matters, too. There's an old adage that states, "*What one generation does in moderation the next will do in excess.*" Our goal as role models to our children and grandchildren is to encourage them to learn good habits by watching our behavior.

Instead of using the phrase, "Do as I say, not as I do," we should be able to say:

- ❍ Yes, you can repeat after me.
- ❍ Yes, you may watch what I'm watching.
- ❍ Yes, you may have a sip of what I'm drinking.
- ❍ Yes, you should follow my lead.

That kind of permission, of course, requires that we live uprightly and passionately for Christ. The apostle Paul reminds us *"... to lead a life worthy of your calling, for you have been called by God"* (Ephesians 4:1, NLT). He is referring to the standard of living according to the Word of God. If we'll pursue Christ and His ways of living, our children and grandchildren will likely follow our lead.

We recently celebrated Christmas together as a family, and we all attended the Christmas Eve service at our church. Our two-year-old granddaughter Joanna sat between my son Jonathon and me. Jonathon was holding Joshua, our five-month-old grandson, and my sister-in-law Julie was holding our ten-month-old granddaughter Tia on her lap next to me. I felt incredibly blessed to all be together!

As we sang Christmas songs, Joanna lifted her little voice in praise, using every syllable she knows. Oh, how precious to hear a child's songs of praise! And as I lifted my hands to worship Jesus, Joanna lifted her hands, too. I have no greater joy than to see my children and grandchildren walk in the love and joy of my Lord. I know that Joanna does not yet have a deep, personal relationship with Christ, but this is how it begins. My mom—Nana—told me many times how I had asked Jesus to come live in my heart when I was three years old, so I know young children have an awareness of Christ long before they can verbalize their understanding. Children's healthy relationships with parents and grandparents help lead them to a healthy relationship with Christ.

But likewise, one of the surest paths to a broken relationship with Christ and with others is hypocritical living. Children are so vulnerable. They learn their patterns of behavior by watching us and behaving as we behave. That's sobering. As much as parents would like to believe that their children will make good choices regardless of patterns they've been given, that usually doesn't happen. We are truly responsible to live consistently in front of our children.

People can typically sense when they're being manipulated or lied to, and children are intuitively even more aware of inconsistencies between words and behavior. Over time, the inconsistency leads to distrust. And parents who are not trustworthy don't foster healthy relationships with their children. As parents (and grandparents), we must behave consistently with our words. Our children are learning about the faithful God we serve by watching us.

Part of creating a culture of *yes* with our children is teaching them to view God rightly—according to His Word. One of the many wonderful qualities of God we see throughout His Word is His generosity toward His children. He often says *yes* to us, His kids. Matthew records the words of Jesus as He sat on a hillside one day teaching His disciples and the crowd of people who had gathered to hear Him:

> *"Keep on asking, and you will receive what you ask for. Keep on seeking, and you will find. Keep on knocking, and the door will be opened to you. For everyone who asks, receives. Everyone who seeks, finds. And to everyone who knocks, the door will be opened. You parents—if your children ask for a loaf of bread, do you give them a stone instead? Or if they ask for a fish, do you give them a snake? Of course not! So if you sinful people know how to give good gifts to your children, how much more will your heavenly Father give good gifts to those who ask him."*
> (Matthew 7:7-11, NLT)

And James, the half-brother of Jesus, instructs us concerning godly wisdom: *"If you need wisdom, ask our generous God and he will give it to you. He will not rebuke you for asking"* (James 1:5, NLT). God provides us the ultimate parenting example in generosity and says *yes* to us often.

Creating a culture of *yes* in our interactions with our children begins with us: our willingness to adjust our schedules, attitudes, and behaviors and living consistent lives that our children can follow.

FOCUS QUESTIONS:

1) How often do you say yes to your children or grandchildren? How often did your parents say yes to you?

2) Think through your daily habits – language you use, shows you watch, music you listen to, and food you eat. Are these habits things that you'd like your children or grandchildren to mimic? If not, what can you change?

PRAYER

Father, help me to accept Your gracious love and generosity toward me so I can be generous toward my children. Help me be attentive to my own negative tendencies so I can change them with the help of Your Holy Spirit.

CPSIA information can be obtained
at www.ICGtesting.com
Printed in the USA
JSHW051954060322
23492JS00006B/22

9 781957 369129